July 13, 1984

To my darling husband, David ~

that this book might be a
source of inspiration to you; that
it will encourage you to stand.
steadfast in your religious convictions
as our father in heaven would want
for you.

Lovingly Yours,

Susan

P.S. I pray always that you will follow
the light of the Lord as I promise
to bear the footprints of your shadow.

Susan.

PUT ON THE WHOLE ARMOR OF GOD

PUT ON THE WHOLE ARMOR OF GOD

LEON R. HARTSHORN

Deseret Book Company   Salt Lake City, Utah 1979

To my wife, Bea

© 1978 by Leon R. Hartshorn
All rights reserved
Printed in the United States of America

Library of Congress Cataloging in Publication Data

Hartshorn, Leon R.
    Put on the whole armor of God.
    Includes index.
    1.   Christian life—Mormon authors.   I.   Title.
BX8656.H37   248′.48′33   78-9473
ISBN 0-87747-709-4

CONTENTS

Chapter 1

BE STRONG
IN THE LORD

Be strong in the Lord,
and in the power of his might.
(Ephesians 6:10.)

I often mentally visualize the deeds of great men and women of The Church of Jesus Christ of Latter-day Saints who lived in the past. It is as though I am there, witnessing the events.

I can see Brigham Young, who has been called to serve a mission for the Church. Weakened by fever, worried and saddened as he leaves his wife and children, he is helped into a wagon. I can see Heber C. Kimball, desperately ill, bidding farewell to his sick wife and children and being assisted into that same wagon.

Heber said, "It appeared to me as though my very inmost parts would melt within me at leaving my family in such a condition." But they had been called by the Lord, through his prophet Joseph Smith, to go to England to take the saving message of the gospel, the "good news" revealed again from the heavens, and go they would, even if earth and hell combined against

1

them. I deeply appreciate their valiance. I deeply appreciate the valiance of their wives Mary Ann Young and Vilate Kimball, each of them ill and each with a new baby.

As they departed, Heber said, "Let's rise up and give them a cheer." They stood up in the wagon and, swinging their hats over their heads, shouted "Hurrah, hurrah for Israel!"

Mary Ann and Vilate, with faith and courage matching that of their husbands, came to the door and cried out, "Goodbye, God bless you."

Brother Heber recalled, "We returned the compliment, and then told the driver to go ahead. After this I felt a spirit of joy and gratitude, having had the satisfaction of seeing my wife standing upon her feet, instead of leaving her in bed, knowing well that I should not see them again for two or three years." (Orson F. Whitney, *The Life of Heber C. Kimball* [Bookcraft, 1967], p. 266.)

I have pondered this story many times and have asked myself, How were they able to do it?

Mentally I have returned to Hiram, Ohio, and relived again and again a brutal attack on the Prophet Joseph Smith. It occurred on a Saturday night in March 1832, while Joseph and his wife and children were living with the John Johnson family. The Prophet and Emma had been up many nights caring for their sick babies—adopted twins, a boy and a girl. It was near midnight when the babies went to sleep. Joseph insisted that Emma go into an adjoining room to get some rest, promising that he would listen for the little ones and take care of them. As he lay down on a trundle bed, fatigue overcame him and he was soon asleep. A mob gathered outside was silently waiting. After the lamps were extinguished and they were certain all were asleep, several men crept into the room where Joseph was sleeping and grabbed him and took him outside. He fought but could not get loose.

The mob carried the Prophet a distance from the

house and tore his clothing from him. They also broke one of his teeth when they tried to force a vial of acid into his mouth; he successfully resisted, and the acid was knocked to the ground. A mobster called for the bucket of tar. Then a man fell on Joseph, scratched him with his fingernails, and cursing, cried out, "G____ D____ ye, that's the way the Holy Ghost falls on folks!"

After covering the Prophet with hot tar, the mob left. Joseph made his way back to the house and called out for help. Emma, opening the door, thought, as she looked at her husband in the dim light of a lamp, that he was covered with blood, and she fainted. When the Prophet called again, Brother Johnson came with a blanket and helped the Prophet and Emma into the house. Other friends came to Joseph's assistance, including a physician, Frederick G. Williams. They worked through the remainder of the night to remove the tar.

The next day the Prophet, despite his tiredness and pain, attended church, preached a sermon, and baptized three persons. (*History of the Church* 1:260-64.)

Joseph Smith, Brigham Young, and Heber C. Kimball and their wives had all entered into covenants with the Lord Jesus Christ. They had taken his name upon them, and they were emulating him in reaching out to save others regardless of the personal sacrifice.

All of us would like to be able to lose ourselves in the service of God and our fellowmen. We would like to "be strong in the Lord."

I have worked with and prayed much for loved ones, friends, and acquaintances whose testimonies have become cold and for whom the joy of service to God and fellowman has been forgotten. I have been surprised, sometimes astonished, at the ones who have fallen, and I miss their hands of fellowship and their former radiant countenances.

No one who is enjoying the sweetness of gospel living would like to join the ranks of the discontented.

May we have confidence that we can endure to the end, or must we live in the shadow of fear that we might also fail?

My heart has been lifted, my soul inspired, and my faith in God increased by the heroic and near-heroic deeds of many fine Latter-day Saints. Not all were heroic; not all were strong. Some were weak, some cowardly, and some vile. When confronted with evil, temptations, trials, and tribulations, some have stood firm and unyielding; others have wavered. Some have fallen, and they are missed.

Our scriptures, as well as our latter-day prophets, testify of the continuing presence and power of evil in the world and of the fact that it will continue to increase on the earth until the second coming of our Lord. President Harold B. Lee said:

> We have some tight places to go before the Lord is through with this church and the world in this dispensation, which is the last dispensation, which shall usher in the coming of the Lord. The gospel was restored to prepare a people ready to receive him. The power of Satan will increase; we see it in evidence on every hand. There will be inroads within the Church. There will be, as President Tanner has said, "Hypocrites, those professing, but secretly are full of dead men's bones." We will see those who profess membership but secretly are plotting and trying to lead people not to follow the leadership that the Lord has set up to preside in this church. (*Conference Report,* October 1970, p. 152.)

The power of Satan is expanding. We are witnesses of it. Books, magazines, movies, and television are being utilized more and more by purveyors of evil. As a result, many of us have grieved at the spiritual loss of friends and loved ones. Although many around them fell, the faithful early Saints were strong in the Lord. How did *they* do it? How can *we* do it? It was not by accident that some fell and some stood, nor has the Lord kept secret the way to be strong. He has given us simple, understandable instructions as to how we can "withstand the evil day."

In Ephesians we have the Lord's word through Paul

to members of the Church at Ephesus. Paul lived in the Roman Empire, was a Roman citizen, and thus was familiar with the powerful Roman army. Apparently thinking of the marvelous Roman armor, the apostle, inspired by the Lord, admonished the saints at Ephesus to put on God's whole armor, his spiritual armor. Spiritual armor will protect all who wear it against the deadly weapons of evil and wickedness.

Paul not only instructed the saints to put on God's whole armor, but he also instructed them as to the specific parts of spiritual armor they must put on:

"Stand therefore, having your loins girt about with truth, and having on the breastplate of righteousness;

"And your feet shod with the preparation of the gospel of peace;

"Above all, taking the shield of faith, wherewith ye shall be able to quench all the fiery darts of the wicked.

"And take the helmet of salvation, and the sword of the Spirit, which is the word of God." (Ephesians 6:14-17.)

One who puts on the whole armor of God and wears it faithfully will be strong in the Lord. Paul is a superb example of his own teachings.

In 1831 the Lord sent an angel to Joseph Smith to forcefully reemphasize the critical need to put on the whole armor of God. Before we can fully comprehend the importance of this latter-day admonition, we must consider the historical background and the first several verses of this very important revelation, section 27 of the Doctrine and Covenants.

In August 1830 the Prophet and his wife, Emma, were residing in Harmony, Pennsylvania. There they were visited by Brother and Sister Newel Knight. The Prophet recorded this event as follows:

Early in the month of August Newel Knight and his wife paid us a visit at my place in Harmony, Pennsylvania; and as neither his wife nor mine had been as yet confirmed, it was proposed that we should confirm them, and partake together of the Sacrament,

5

before he and his wife should leave us. In order to prepare for this I set out to procure some wine for the occasion, but had gone only a short distance when I was met by a heavenly messenger, and received the following revelation.... (*History of the Church* 1:106.)

The angel, representing the Lord and speaking for the Lord, instructed the Prophet concerning the sacrament: "For, behold, I say unto you, that it mattereth not what ye shall drink when ye partake of the sacrament, if it so be that ye do it with an eye single to my glory...." (D&C 27:2.)

From that time bread and water, instead of wine, have generally been used as the emblems of the sacrament, symbolically representing the flesh and blood of our Savior. The heavenly messenger also informed the Prophet that wine should not be purchased from his enemies and that the saints should partake of none except it "is made new among you." (D&C 27:4.)

The Lord then declared that the hour was approaching when he would return to the earth and drink of the fruit of the vine. That is, he would partake of the sacrament with Joseph and with all of the great leaders of his kingdom, and he enumerated many, especially those who had had a part in the restoration of all things in the dispensation of the fulness of times. Moroni, Elias, John the Baptist, Elijah, Joseph who was sold into Egypt, Jacob, Isaac, Abraham, Adam, Peter, James, and John were all mentioned by name. (D&C 27:5-13.)

In addition to these, each of us, if we desire and if we are worthy, may be present and also partake of the sacrament on this magnificent occasion. (D&C 27:14.)

When we partake of the sacrament, we have the privilege of renewing our covenants. President John Taylor stated that as we partake of the sacrament we are also foreshadowing the future time when we will be in the presence of our Savior:

We have met to partake of the Sacrament of the Lord's Supper, ... for in partaking of the Sacrament we not only commemorate the death and sufferings of our Lord and Savior Jesus Christ, but we also shadow forth the time when he will come again and when we shall meet and eat bread with him in the kingdom of God. When we are thus assembled together, we may expect to receive guidance and blessings from God. (*Journal of Discourses* 14:185.)

In Matthew 26:26-30 Jesus told his disciples that the next time he partook of the sacrament would be with his faithful followers at his coming. Joseph Fielding Smith, commenting on these verses, said:

The Savior informed his Apostles on the night he ate the Passover that he would not drink of the "fruit of the vine" with them again, until he should "drink it new with them in the kingdom of God." This was reiterated in the revelation to Joseph Smith, wherein the Lord promised to drink and eat with his prophets and saints, in his Father's kingdom which shall be built up on the earth. (*Church History and Modern Revelation* [Deseret Book, 1953], 1:132-33.)

When the Lord comes in his glory we will honor him. The words of a well-known hymn seem appropriate in describing the joy of this future event:

Come, ye children of the Lord, Let us sing with one accord;
Let us raise a joyful strain To our Lord who soon will reign
On this earth, when it shall be Cleansed from all iniquity;
When all men from sin will cease, And will live in love and peace.

O how joyful it will be, When our Savior we shall see!
When in splendor he'll descend, Then all wickedness will end.
O what songs we then will sing To our Savior, Lord and King!
O what love will then bear sway, When our fears shall flee away!

All arrayed in spotless white, We will dwell 'mid truth and light;
We will sing the songs of praise, We will shout in joyous lays.

7

Earth shall then be cleansed from sin. Ev'ry living thing
   therein
Shall in love and beauty dwell; Then with joy each heart
   will swell.
                                        —Hymns, no. 23

We in this dispensation have been given the commission to extend an invitation to the inhabitants of the
earth to repent and prepare themselves to receive and
live the principles of the gospel, to receive the blessings
of the Lord in this life, at his coming, during the millen-
nium, and throughout all eternity. We cannot effectively
extend that joyous invitation unless we do as he has
instructed us through his prophets in all dispensations.
In his instructions to Joseph Smith, the angel declared,
in words similar to Paul's:

> Wherefore, lift up your hearts and rejoice, and gird up your
> loins, and take upon you my whole armor, that ye may be able to
> withstand the evil day, having done all, that ye may be able to
> stand.
> Stand, therefore, having your loins girt about with truth, hav-
> ing on the breastplate of righteousness, and your feet shod with the
> preparation of the gospel of peace which I have sent mine angels to
> commit unto you.
> Taking the shield of faith wherewith ye shall be able to quench
> all the fiery darts of the wicked;
> And take the helmet of salvation, and the sword of my spirit,
> which I will pour out upon you, and my word which I reveal unto
> you. . . . (D&C 27:16-18.)

How were Joseph Smith, Brigham Young, Heber C.
Kimball, and many others able to demonstrate such
faith and courage and bring many souls to the Lord?
They wore the whole armor of God.

The scriptures and the history of the Church are
filled with the names of those who put on the whole
armor of God, and we rejoice over them. In the scriptures and in the pages of Church history are also
recorded the names of many who either did not put on
the whole armor of God or who did not keep his whole

armor on, and we grieve over them. We are to put on the whole armor of God so we can be strong in the Lord and in the power of his might, and be victorious in the great battle of life, the battle for the souls of men.

Chapter 2

THE BATTLE IS REAL

For we wrestle not against flesh and blood, but against principalities, against powers, against the rulers of darkness of this world, against spiritual wickedness in high places. (Ephesians 6:12.)

The date was February 16, 1832; the place, Hiram, Ohio. The Prophet Joseph Smith and Sidney Rigdon had not understood a reference in the Bible concerning the resurrection of the just and the unjust, so they inquired of the Lord. A glorious vision was opened to them, which they described as follows:

And we beheld the glory of the Son, on the right hand of the Father, and received of his fulness;

And saw the holy angels, and them who are sanctified before his throne, worshiping God, and the Lamb, who worship him forever and ever.

And now, after the many testimonies which have been given of him, this is the testimony, last of all, which we give of him: That he lives!

For we saw him, even on the right hand of God; and we heard the voice bearing record that he is the Only Begotten of the Father—

That by him, and through him, and of him, the worlds are and were created, and the inhabitants thereof are begotten sons and daughters unto God. (D&C 76:20-24.)

Joseph and Sidney had the sacred privilege of beholding the Father and the Son and seeing holy angels worshiping them. They beheld as well as heard that our Lord Jesus Christ is the Only Begotten in the flesh. They learned that by him and through him and of him the worlds are, and that we are sons and daughters of God. All mankind has a Father in heaven, and Jesus Christ is our Savior.

Next Joseph and Sidney beheld a most sobering scene. They saw that an angel of God, one who was in the presence of God, rebelled against the Only Begotten Son whom the Father loved, and was thrust down from the presence of God and the Son. The heavens lamented and wept over him, for Lucifer, a son of the morning, had fallen. Joseph Smith and Sidney Rigdon apparently saw Lucifer in vision as clearly as they saw the Father and the Son.

And this we saw also, and bear record, that an angel of God who was in authority in the presence of God, who rebelled against the Only Begotten Son whom the Father loved and who was in the bosom of the Father, was thrust down from the presence of God and the Son.

And was called Perdition, for the heavens wept over him—he was Lucifer, a son of the morning.

And we beheld, and lo, he is fallen! is fallen, even a son of the morning!

And while we were yet in the Spirit, the Lord commanded us that we should write the vision; for we beheld Satan, that old serpent, even the devil, who rebelled against God, and sought to take the kingdom of our God and his Christ—

Wherefore, he maketh war with the saints of God, and encompasseth them round about. (D&C 76:25-29.)

Lucifer, or the devil, is real, and the one-third of the hosts of heaven who were cast down to the earth with him are also real. The Lord, speaking further on this subject, said, "For, behold, the devil was before Adam, for he rebelled against me, saying, Give me thine honor, which is my power; and also a third part of the hosts of heaven turned he away from me because of their agency; And they were thrust down, and thus became the devil and his angels." (D&C 29:36-37.)

Later, when the First Presidency was organized, Sidney became Joseph Smith's first counselor. Yet, at the death of the Prophet, Sidney literally was encompassed round about by Satan. It was done so subtly that he didn't know he was wrong or that he was being influenced by the evil one. He imitated Satan and tried to usurp authority not his by presenting himself as the guardian of the Church and opposing the Lord's chosen twelve. Yes, Satan encompassed Sidney. Sidney Rigdon's intentions were not bad; he was simply deceived, and thereby he lost his standing in the Church.

Peter wisely counseled: "Be sober, be vigilant; because your adversary the devil, as a roaring lion, walketh about, seeking whom he may devour. . . ." (1 Peter 5:8.)

Peace-loving people do not want war—they use all honorable means to avoid it. But if an enemy insists on attacking, insists on making war, peace-loving people have war. It is not of their choosing, but they have war. We as Latter-day Saints have war; it is not of our choosing, but we are in a battle. The struggle is not for lands or wealth, but for souls, eternal children of our Father in heaven, souls of infinite value.

Lucifer, the son of the morning, was so filled with pride and arrogance in premortal life that he would stop at nothing to usurp the kingdom of his Father, a perfect being. He continues that struggle here on the earth. President George Q. Cannon wrote:

It is the supremacy of this earth that is being contended for. Satan is determined that God shall not have this earth and He shall not reign here; he is determined in this, and if he could he would shed the blood of every man and woman on the face of the earth rather than it should go into the hands of God. All those who are connected with him would, if they could, slay every man that stands in their pathway.

The more faithful a man is in the cause of God the more the hatred of the wicked is manifested against him. (Jerreld L. Newquist, comp., *Gospel Truth* [Deseret Book, 1974], 2:41-42.)

Reality may not always be pleasant, but ignorance of the truth could be devastating. Our prophets have been careful to warn us, instruct us, and prepare us concerning our enemy. From President Wilford Woodruff we learn:

> . . . one third of the hosts of heaven were cast out. . . . I say to my counselors, to the apostles, to the seventies, the high priests, the bishops, and all men who bear the Holy Priesthood, do you suppose these devils are around us without trying to do something? I say to my brethren who bear the priesthood, we have got a mighty warfare to wage with these spirits. We cannot escape it. What will they do to you? They will try to make us do anything and everything that is not right. (G. Homer Durham, ed., *Discourses of Wilford Woodruff* [Bookcraft, 1946], pp. 239-40.)

We are further counseled by President Brigham Young:

> Shall we have a warfare? We shall; we will war and contend for the right, and trust in our God until righteousness is established upon the earth, until peace shall reign everywhere. . . . What, then, is the mission of Satan, that common foe of all the children of men? it is to destroy and make desolate. (*Journal of Discourses* 11:239-40.)

The teachings of the scriptures and of the prophets concerning Satan are clear. He is totally evil, vile, and corrupt. He cannot be trusted ever, in any way. He is the father of all lies, the master of deceit. He is cunning, and whatever he needs to say or do to confuse a person and lead him astray, he will do. To him everything is fair, because there is not any good in him.

We must understand our enemy and respect his ability. He is brilliantly evil, and his plan to increase evil in the world is also brilliant. We must never underestimate him. He uses pleasing words if it meets his purposes. He also acts the part of a gentleman if it meets his purposes. He flatters to deceive and to overcome. If we are not vigilant and if we permit him, he will lead us "carefully down to hell."

President Cannon succinctly characterizes Satan:

We have a foe opposed to us that is the most wily, that is the most cunning, that is the most determined, that is the most unscrupulous, that can be imagined, and that foe is one who was once a great angel holding authority in the presence of God. He was our brother, sitting side by side with our Redeemer, having equal opportunities with Him. But he rebelled. He turned against the Father, because he could not have his own way. He determined that he would overthrow the throne of his Father, and engaged in a rebellion to destroy his plans. . . . We have this kind of a foe to contend against. (*Journal of Discourses* 25:301-2.)

Satan is an apostate from truth and light. He knew truth and light, he was blessed by it, and he rejected it. That is why he can do so much damage. He knows our Father in heaven and he knows our Lord and Savior Jesus Christ. He therefore knows how to pervert the truth and cast doubts in a most diabolical way. The most deadly enemy is a fallen former friend and confidant.

If Satan had not been one of us, a trusted one in a high position of authority, he would not now be such a cunning foe. An enemy in wartime may be powerful and awesome, but the treacherous defector who becomes an enemy is more to be feared and much more difficult to combat because he possesses knowledge that was never intended for an enemy to possess.

Satan is a bitter, vindictive, evil apostate. His ego, his conceit, and his pride led him into the greatest of all follies. He believed that pride and power could establish him as a God, but he was unwilling to meet the requirements for Godhood. That is, he was unwilling to exercise faith and self-control, make sacrifices, and endure the hardships from which godly qualities are developed.

Lucifer wanted to be a god, but he was not willing to pay the price. He tried to overthrow the Father—the height of ingratitude, disloyalty, and unfaithfulness. He tried desperately to believe his own lie—that he is really the only begotten son of God.

One of those whom he tried unsuccessfully to deceive was Moses:

> And it came to pass that when Moses had said these words, behold, Satan came tempting him, saying: Moses, son of man, worship me. . . . And again Moses said; I will not cease to call upon God, I have other things to inquire of him: for his glory has been upon me, wherefore I can judge between him and thee. Depart hence, Satan, And now, when Moses had said these words, Satan cried with a loud voice, and rent upon the earth, and commanded, saying: I am the Only Begotten, worship me. . . .
>
> And now Satan began to tremble, and the earth shook; and Moses received strength, and called upon God, saying: In the name of the Only Begotten, depart hence, Satan.
>
> And it came to pass that Satan cried with a loud voice, with weeping, and wailing, and gnashing of teeth, and he departed hence, even from the presence of Moses, that he beheld him not. (Moses 1:12, 18-22.)

Satan, an apostate from truth and light, is a bully. He picks on, afflicts, and torments the weak. How totally different he is from his Father and from his brother Jesus Christ, the true Lord and Savior. Satan, the destroyer, is the personification of evil, and our Lord Jesus Christ, the Savior, is the personification of good.

Joseph Smith, after being shocked for the third time as he tried to obtain the gold plates from the Hill Cumorah, cried out, "Why can I not obtain this book?" I do not think he expected an answer, but he received one. The ancient guardian of the plates stood before him and said, "Because you have not kept the commandments of the Lord." He had not remembered the instructions of the previous night. Joseph sought God's forgiveness, and soon "his mind and soul were enlightened as they had been the night before, and he was filled with the Holy Spirit." The heavens were opened, and the glory of the Lord shone around about and rested upon him. As he gazed, enthralled, Moroni directed his attention to another vision, saying, "Look." As Joseph turned, he was shown a vision of Satan and his followers. He was permitted to see the great contrast between the power of God and the power of Satan. Then the angel said:

> All this is shown, the good and the evil, the holy and the impure, the glory of God and the power of darkness, that ye may know hereafter the two powers and never be influenced or overcome by that wicked one. Behold, whatever entices and leads to good and to do good, is of God, and whatever does not is of that wicked one: it is he that fills the hearts of men with evil, to walk in darkness and blaspheme God; and you may learn from henceforth, that his ways are to destruction, but the way of holiness is peace and rest. . . . You have now beheld the power of God manifested and the power of Satan; you see that there is nothing that is desirable in the works of darkness; that they cannot bring happiness: that those who are overcome herewith are miserable, while on the other hand the righteous are blessed with a place in the kingdom of God where joy unspeakable surrounds them. . . . (Francis W. Kirkham, *A New Witness for Christ in America* [Brigham Young University, 1960], 1:97-98.)

What a startling lesson—a lesson that never diminished in vividness during the life of Joseph Smith.

Joseph's mother recalled this event and said of it:

> The angel showed him, by contrast, the difference between good and evil, and likewise the consequences of both obedience and disobedience to the commandments of God, in such a striking manner, that the impression was always vivid in his memory until the very end of his days; and in giving a relation of this circumstance, not long prior to his death, he remarked, that ever afterwards he was willing to keep the commandments of God. (Lucy Mack Smith, *History of the Prophet Joseph Smith, by His Mother* [Bookcraft, 1958], p. 81.)

In less than twenty-four hours Joseph Smith had seen the angel Moroni five times, and each time he had spoken to him at length. He had seen the ancient gold plates, the glory of the heavens, and also Satan and his associates.

The contrast, the astonishing difference between good and evil, comes into sharp focus when we view the personality, attributes, and deeds of our Lord Jesus Christ on the one hand and the personality, attributes, and deeds of the devil on the other hand.

17

By their fruits shall ye know them. The fruits of our Lord would be instantly recognizable as coming from him—love, kindness, humility, goodness, joy. The evil fruits of Satan—hopelessness, despair, hate, lust, pride, wickedness—are as readily identifiable.

If one persists in righteousness, he can become like our Savior. If one persists in evil intensely enough, he can become like the devil. This has been demonstrated from the beginning. One son of Adam, Seth, is called "a perfect man." (D&C 107:43.) Another son, Cain, became like Satan. (Moses 5.)

Yes, the battle for men's souls is real. Jesus has given us the following concerning the importance of saving souls:

Remember the worth of souls is great in the sight of God;

For, behold, the Lord your Redeemer suffered death in the flesh; wherefore he suffered the pain of all men, that all men might repent and come unto him.

And he hath risen again from the dead, that he might bring all men unto him, on conditions of repentance.

And how great is his joy in the soul that repenteth!

Wherefore, you are called to cry repentance unto this people.

And if it so be that you should labor all your days in crying repentance unto this people, and bring, save it be one soul unto me, how great shall be your joy with him in the kingdom of my Father!

And now, if your joy will be great with one soul that you have brought unto me into the kingdom of my Father, how great will be your joy if you should bring many souls unto me! (D&C 18:10-16.)

It is clear that we have to fight an enemy to save our own souls and the souls of others. We will do it, and we will do it joyfully because we love our Father in heaven and our Lord and Savior Jesus Christ and our fellow beings. In order to succeed in the battle we must put on the whole armor of God.

Chapter 3

THE ARMOR OF TRUTH

Stand, therefore, having your loins girt about with truth. (*Ephesians 6:14; D&C 27:16.*)

The first part of the armor mentioned by Paul in his epistle to the Ephesians is also the first part of the armor mentioned by the angel in this dispensation, the girdle of armor about the loins, the armor of truth.

In response to a question from Pilate, Jesus declared: "To this end was I born, and for this cause came I into the world, that I should bear witness unto the truth. Every one that is of the truth heareth my voice. Pilate saith unto him, What is truth? . . ." (John 18:37-38.)

What is truth? Jesus did not answer the question. The answer is not given in the Bible. However, it is revealed to us by the Lord in the Doctrine and Covenants: "And truth is knowledge of things as they are, and as they were, and as they are to come; And whatsoever is more or less than this is the spirit of that wicked one who was a liar from the beginning." (D&C 93:24-25.)

Jesus testified, "I am the way, the truth, and the life.
. . ." (John 14:6.) Our Savior, who desires all to know
the truth, taught his disciples: "If ye continue in my
word, then are ye my disciples indeed; And ye shall
know the truth, and the truth shall make you free."
(John 8:31-32.)

Truth shall make us free—free from doubt, free
from fear, free from sin. The Lord, who loves all of us,
is no respecter of persons. He desires all of us to know
the truth, which is his gospel.

Richard O. Clark shared with me a story that I have
pondered many times. He and his companion knocked
on the door of an attic apartment in Germany. There
was no response. Not to be denied, one of them took a
broom that was standing in the hallway and pounded
on the door with the broom handle. The door was
opened, and "oh, how the little lady inside needed the
truth." She had lost her husband and all ten of her
children in World War II. She was alone. She rejoiced
in the true gospel message and in a short time joyfully
entered the waters of baptism. Imagine how the truth
must have lifted her burden of sorrow and grief as she
heard the words of eternal life. (*Inspirational Missionary
Stories* [Deseret Book, 1976], pp. 1-3.)

The Lord would like everyone to hear, understand,
and rejoice. That is why he and his true servants teach
his gospel simply.

Brigham Young explained why Joseph Smith was
such a great teacher:

The excellency of the glory of the character of brother Joseph
Smith was that he could reduce heavenly things to the understanding of the finite. When he preached to the people—revealed the
things of God, the will of God, the plan of salvation, the purposes
of Jehovah, the relation in which we stand to him and all the
heavenly beings, he reduced his teachings to the capacity of every
man, woman, and child, making them as plain as a well-defined
pathway. This should have convinced every person that ever heard
of him or his divine authority and power, for no other man was
able to teach as he could, and no person can reveal the things of
God, but by the revelations of Jesus Christ. When we hear a man

20

that can speak of heavenly things, and present them to the people in a way that they can be understood, you may know that to that man the avenue is open, and that he, by some power, has communication with heavenly beings; and when the highest intelligence is exhibited, he, perhaps, has communication with the highest intelligence that exists. (*Journal of Discourses* 8:206.)

Joseph Smith's brother Hyrum instructs us to teach the basic principles of the gospel:

We have every power and principle to teach the people. Say what God says, and say no more. Never deviate one fraction from what God tells you. . . . Give out the simple principles. A man never fails who only says what he knows; and if any man says more, and can't give reasons, he falls short. Preach the first principles of the Gospel—preach them over again; you will find that day after day new ideas and additional light concerning them will be revealed to you. You can enlarge upon them so as to comprehend them clearly. You will then be able to make them more plainly understood by those who teach, so that you will meet with scarcely any honest man but who will obey them, and none who can oppose. (*History of the Church* 6:323.)

While here on the earth Jesus taught simply. Peter and James, fishermen, had little difficulty understanding the principles he explained. Matthew, a tax collector, understood the Savior's message and left his tax table and followed him.

In our day the Savior continues to communicate simply, as is illustrated by the following incident taken from the history of the Church.

Joseph Smith presented a number of revelations to a small group of priesthood bearers, and then proposed that these revelations become a new book of scripture. The brethren were hesitant, because to them, the revelations didn't sound like the Lord. Joseph, not being able to answer their objections, suggested that they ask the Lord. This is the direct answer from God:

Behold, I am God and have spoke it; these commandments are of me, and were given unto my servants in their weakness, after the manner of their language, that they might come to understanding.

And inasmuch as they erred it might be made known;

And inasmuch as they sought wisdom they might be instructed;

And inasmuch as they sinned they might be chastened, that they might repent;

And inasmuch as they were humble they might be made strong, and blessed from on high, and receive knowledge from time to time. (D&C 1:24-28.)

This is just what we would expect of our loving Lord. He wants us to be able to understand and to know the truth so that we may be free. Even after this revelation was received, William E. McLellin was not satisfied, so the Prophet inquired of the Lord again, and the revelation that was given is a superb example of the principle the Lord has just revealed.

Your eyes have been upon my servant Joseph Smith, Jun., and his language you have known, . . . and you have sought in your hearts knowledge that you might express beyond his language; this you also know.

Now, seek ye out of the Book of Commandments, even the least that is among them, and appoint him that is the most wise among you;

Or, if there be any among you that shall make one like unto it, then ye are justified in saying that ye do not know that they are true;

But if ye cannot make one like unto it, ye are under condemnation if ye do not bear record that they are true. (D&C 67:5-8.)

What could be more simple? William E. McLellin, of course, could not write a revelation and so he repented. (See Joseph Fielding Smith, *Essentials in Church History* [Deseret Book, 1967], p. 119.)

Joseph F. Smith, a great prophet and gospel teacher, said:

One thing about this so-called philosophy of religion that is very undesirable lies in the fact that as soon as we convert our religion into a system of philosophy, none but philosophers can understand, appreciate, or enjoy it. God, in his revelation to man, has made his word so simple that the humblest of men, without special training, may enjoy great faith, comprehend the teachings of the gospel, and enjoy undisturbed their religious convictions. (*Gospel Doctrine* [Deseret Book, 1963], pp. 8-9.)

On another occasion this latter-day prophet said, "It is, therefore, of great importance that the gospel should be preached in the simplest and most intelligible way." (Ibid., p. 359.) He further taught: "To the faithful Latter-day Saints is given the right to know the truth, as God knows it." (Ibid., p. 6.)

I am thoroughly persuaded that truth is simple and that the true gospel is not complex; it is simple to those who receive it and obey it. To a virtuous woman the principle of being virtuous is simple, easy to understand. For her the standard of conduct is always the same, regardless of where she is or whom she is with.

The principle of tithing is simple; we pay one-tenth of our income. Any little child can understand it. Tithing becomes complex only when we do not pay it. To the tithe payer, regardless of his level of income, the principle is simple and easy to understand. To the nontithe payer, regardless of his level of income, the principle is complex and difficult to understand.

Simplicity is a companion to obedience, while complexity is a companion to disobedience. To the person who always tells the truth, there is nothing complex about that; he just simply tells the truth in all situations. It is the telling of lies that brings complexity into one's life. He must now remember which lies he has told and to whom he has told them, so that he can tell the same lie again to the same person.

Sin always brings complexity and confusion. Obedience is simple, while disobedience is complex. If, then, a gospel principle seems complex, we should view it again from the vantage point of obedience, and the apparent complexity will soon disappear.

Elder Neal A. Maxwell has given us these exceptional insights:

It is true today; the simpleness, the easiness of the gospel is such that it causes people to perish because they can't receive it. We like variety. We like intellectual embroidery. We like complexity. I think we like complexity at times because it gives us an excuse for failure, that is, as you increase the complexity of a belief system, you provide more and more refuges for those who don't want to comply; you thereby increase the number of excuses that people can make for failure to comply, and you create a sophisticated intellectual structure which causes people to talk about the gospel instead of doing it. . . . But the gospel of Jesus Christ really is not complex. It strips us of any basic excuse for compliance, and yet many of us are forever trying to make it more complex. ("The Simplicity of the Gospel," *BYU Speeches of the Year,* May 4, 1969, p. 6.)

President Joseph F. Smith said: ". . . if we depart from the simplicity of God's word . . . we become the victims of vanity. . . . The religion of the heart, the unaffected and simple communion which we should hold with God, is the highest safeguard of the Latter-day Saints." (*Gospel Doctrine,* p. 9.)

All truth is of our Lord Jesus Christ, and the Holy Ghost is called the Spirit of truth. If we desire the Lord's blessings and the witness of the Holy Ghost, we must speak truth, teach truth, and live by truth. No other standard is acceptable. Living better than the majority of the people about us is not how we determine our behavior.

We may live much better than the majority of people, and still be below the standard of truth.

It might be revealing if each of us asked ourself, Are the television programs I now watch, the movies I now view, the books and magazines I now read, below the standard of what I used to watch and read? Would I have watched a movie or a television program like this five years ago or ten years ago? I should be more righteous than I was five years ago or ten years ago. I should have progressed toward perfection. Have I?

Perfection is a process that should be improved as the years go by. It may be a little difficult to accurately judge our progress, or lack of it, if we measure ourselves by the standard of the worldly society around us. We must be certain that we are judging ourselves by God's absolute standard of truth and not a relative standard of the world. For example, if ten years ago our taste was more discriminating than that of 70 percent of the moviegoers, and today it is more discriminating than, say, 90 percent, do we rationalize and think we are doing well because our relative position has improved? It is actually possible that our absolute position may have moved substantially downward, if we now tolerate things we would not have tolerated five or ten years ago.

Perhaps we ought to turn to the thirteenth Article of Faith and let its truths sink into our souls: "We believe in being honest, true, chaste, benevolent, virtuous, and in doing good to all men; indeed, we may say that we follow the admonition of Paul—We believe all things, we hope all things, we have endured many things, and hope to be able to endure all things. If there is anything virtuous, lovely, or of good report or praiseworthy, we seek after these things."

Paul and the angel who appeared to Joseph Smith both said, "Stand, therefore, having your loins girt about with truth." The Roman armor that protected the loins was held in place by a belt. The armor was made of overlapping pieces so that it was flexible and would not inhibit the soldier's movement. The spiritual armor spoken of by the Lord protects one's virtue, and that which protects virtue is truth, or true knowledge.

One of our sons, who was desirous of going on a mission, returned from his interview with our stake president. As he walked through the front door and sat down, I thought, "This is the happiest face I have ever seen." I commented on it. "You're happy, aren't you." His reply was, "Dad, I don't know if you can know just how happy I am." "Why are you so happy?" "Oh!" he said, "I just can't express how happy it made me to be able to look my stake president straight in the eyes and answer all those questions the way they should be answered."

"I am happy that you answered all the questions the right way, and I am very pleased that you are morally clean. I know that some of your acquaintances aren't. Why are you?"

He thought for a moment and then said, "It is my knowledge." It was his gospel knowledge that had protected him.

President Harold B. Lee taught that "truth is to be the substance of which the girdle about your loins is to be formed if your virtue and vital strength is to be safeguarded. . . ." (*Stand Ye in Holy Places* [Deseret Book, 1974], p. 331.)

What, then, does the armor of truth about the loins protect? It protects one's virtue, one's chastity. When we are confronted by temptations, it is truth that overcomes the temptations, for when we know the truth, temptation can be seen for what it is—error, falsehood, wrongdoing, sin.

Joseph who was sold into Egypt lived to become one of the greatest servants and prophets of the Lord in the history of the world. We are thrilled when we read in the book of Genesis of his greatness of soul; we are inspired by his prophecies in the Book of Mormon (2 Nephi 3); and we are impressed with his courage in youth when he had the strength to resist evil. As Potiphar's wife approached him, Joseph did not rationalize; he did not attempt to justify a wrong; he did not give the situation a falsely respectable title. He knew the truth and he lived by it. He declared, "How then can I do this great wickedness, and sin against God?" (Genesis 39:9.)

Joseph had the spiritual armor of truth fastened securely about his loins. He fled from the presence of evil. He paid some worldly consequences for knowing the truth and for living by true principles and protecting his virtue. Though he was imprisoned, the day came when he triumphantly returned as a high official in the Egyptian government. Because of his unwavering allegiance to truth he was able to save himself and his family from famine and possible starvation. He also saved the entire Egyptian nation. It is likely that Potiphar and his sinful wife were among those who were saved. His strength was a blessing to the very one who attempted to cause his downfall.

President Joseph F. Smith taught that "sometimes in life, we are brought face to face with an enemy whose evil ways are beyond our power of combat, a victory over which cannot be hoped for. There is only one escape from moral annihilation and that is in retreat." (*Gospel Doctrine,* p. 374.)

Evil is overcome by standing steadfast and contending against it. At other times one's welfare is enhanced by leaving the situation. We should seek to be wise and to have God's guidance so that we can make correct choices in all of life's situations.

George Q. Cannon wrote concerning truth:

> It is those who cling to the truth who become victors in every conflict, either in a small circle or upon a large scale. False gods, false religion, false worship, false doctrine, false conduct cannot save the least human being. Error may triumph for a while, but its triumph is only temporary. The man who possesses the truth and will abide by it and cling to it will most assuredly, whatever conflicts he may have and evil influences to contend with, be ultimately victorious. (*Gospel Truth* 2:3.)

To overcome the lures and entrapments of wicked ones, we must know the truth and be able to instantly and firmly label evil, evil—not adult, sophisticated, mature, funny, or clever, but evil. If it is evil, we should call it that, and, in addition, know exactly the consequences of a sinful act, and just what will be traded for the evil if we indulge in it. Sin cannot bring happiness or freedom. It can only result in misery. One who knows the truth will not trade present as well as future joy, present as well as future opportunity, for a brief moment of giving way to unrighteous desires.

"It was my knowledge," our son said—true knowledge! It was the spiritual armor of truth about his loins that protected his virtue and brought great joy to himself and his loved ones and to many others to whom he brought the truth.

Truth that is internalized becomes the armor about the loins that protects one's virtue. The importance of chastity cannot be overstated. The scriptures record: "For behold, many of the daughters of the Lamanites have they taken prisoners; and after depriving them of that which was most dear and precious above all things, which is chastity and virtue." (Moroni 9:9.) And again: "For I, the Lord God, delight in the chastity of women. And whoredoms are an abomination before me; thus saith the Lord of Hosts." (Jacob 2:28.)

Among those who will inherit the telestial kingdom are the adulterers, whoremongers, and, in the context of this subject, "whosoever loves and makes a lie." (D&C 76:103.) "These are they who are thrust down to hell." (D&C 76:84.) President Spencer W. Kimball has warned us against immorality:

> Infidelity is one of the great sins of our generation. The movies, the books, the magazine stories all seem to glamorize the faithlessness of husbands and wives. *Nothing is holy,* not even marriage vows. The unfaithful woman is the heroine and is justified, and the hero is so built up that he can do no wrong. It reminds us of Isaiah who said: "Wo unto those who call evil good, and good evil. . . ." (Isaiah 5:20.)
>
> We make no apology then for raising our voices loud to a world that is ripening in sin. The Lord has said: "Say nothing but repentance unto this generation. . . ." (D&C 6:9.)
>
> The adversary is subtle; he is cunning, he knows that he cannot induce good men and women immediately to do major evils so he moves slyly, whispering half truths until he has his intended victims following him, and finally he clamps his chains upon them and fetters them tight, and then he laughs at their discomfiture and their misery. (*Conference Report,* October 1962, p. 56. Italics in original.)

The Lord has given us the sacred power to have children. One of Satan's major deceptions is that it is not wrong to misuse this power. This is a terrible, destructive, life-shattering lie.

We wear the spiritual armor of truth about our loins

to protect our chastity, our virtue. Great is the sorrow of those who do not put this part of God's armor on and keep it on. But for those who do, how great is their re-joicing. We not only rejoice in receiving the truth of our Lord and Savior Jesus Christ, but we joyfully sing of it.

Oh say, what is truth? 'Tis the fairest gem
That the riches of worlds can produce,
And priceless the value of truth will be when
The proud monarch's costliest diadem
Is counted but dross and refuse.

Yes, say, what is truth? 'Tis the brightest prize
To which mortals or Gods can aspire;
Go search in the depths where it glittering lies
Or ascend in pursuit to the loftiest skies:
'Tis an aim for the noblest desire.

The sceptre may fall from the despot's grasp
When with winds of stern justice he copes,
But the pillar of truth will endure to the last,
And its firm rooted bulwarks outstand the rude blast,
And the wreck of the fell tyrant's hopes.

Then say, what is truth? 'Tis the last and the first,
For the limits of time it steps o'er.
Though the heavens depart and the earth's fountains
*   burst,*
Truth, the sum of existence, will weather the worst,
Eternal, unchanged, evermore.
                    —*Hymns*, no. 143

"I glory in plainness; I glory in truth; I glory in my Jesus. . . ." (2 Nephi 33:6.)

Chapter 4

THE BREASTPLATE OF RIGHTEOUSNESS

Having . . . the breastplate of righteousness.
(Ephesians 6:14; D&C 27:16.)

If an enemy arrow or the tip of an enemy sword had pierced a Roman soldier's heart, it probably would have been a fatal wound. Such a risk could not be taken, so the soldier wore a breastplate of protective armor that covered his chest completely. We too must protect ourselves today.

There is no ultimate success for God's work on the earth without a people who are pure in heart. No unclean person can enter God's presence; one who is unclean cannot know the love, peace, and joy that come from possessing a pure heart.

If one cannot successfully fulfill his mission on earth unless he achieves a condition of having a pure heart, then he would be foolish indeed if he did not put on the "breastplate of righteousness" which protects the heart.

Righteousness means meeting the standards of what is morally right and just. A righteous person has integrity. He does not compromise himself. He is perfectly honest in all his activities.

One returned missionary who had not attended missionary reunions for several years received an invitation to a special reunion. The invitation stated: "It has been twenty-five years since the President and his wife served in the mission field. Please be a part of an evening set aside to honor them."

As the returned missionary sat by his wife and listened once more to the dynamic voice of his mission president, his mind wandered back through the years to a missionary conference in a small chapel in the mission field. It was late, and the conference had filled the day and lasted into the night. The last missionary had borne his testimony and the president was going to close the meeting, but first he would bear his testimony.

He spoke of his youth and young adulthood in a western community, of his studies at an eastern university, of his schoolwork, friends, and athletics, and the influence of a highly respected coach. He also told the missionaries about a bad habit he had developed almost unconsciously, one that had come so subtly that he hardly realized he had it. The bad habit was listening to and telling dirty stories and jokes.

After graduation he returned to the West, where he married and established his profession. He continued to be active in the Church as he had always been. One night he had a dream. He said he knew that there were many different types of dreams—some from eating too much pie, and some from God, as indicated in the scriptures. This dream was from the Lord.

He said, "In my dream I found myself entering the door of our chapel. As I looked toward the pulpit, a brilliant light began to appear above the pulpit. A glorious heavenly being was descending in the midst of that light. I realized that I was beholding my Lord and Savior, Jesus Christ. I had loved him, worshiped him, and served him from my childhood, and now for the first time I had the privilege of being in his presence. He looked at me and our eyes met. He called me by name and said, 'Turn your head, for you are not worthy to behold Me.' I was crushed. I dropped my eyes and turned my head. Then the light in the room gradually disappeared, and I was standing in darkness. I awoke, got up from my bed, and began to pace the floor. I didn't know why I was unworthy to behold my Lord, but I knew I was.

"Days passed, then weeks. I continued to ponder and pray. One evening when I returned from work I picked up the Bible. It fell open at Matthew, chapter five, where we find the Sermon on the Mount and the Beatitudes. I read: 'Blessed are they which do hunger and thirst after righteousness: for they shall be filled. Blessed are the merciful: for they shall obtain mercy.' (Matthew 5:6-7.) Then my eyes fell upon this verse: 'Blessed are the pure in heart: for they shall see God.' (Matthew 5:8.) I then knew why I was not worthy to behold my Lord. I was not pure in heart."

The president raised up on his tiptoes and lifted a clenched fist high into the air, then brought it down hard on the pulpit, the sound splitting the silence in the room. He declared, "I have not listened to nor told a dirty joke or story from that day to this." He lifted his fist into the air and again slammed it down on the pulpit with great force as he added, "As long as I live, I never will."

The returned missionary's mind returned to the present. He said to himself, "President, if given the opportunity, I could now say to you that you so impressed me those many years ago when I heard you relate that sacred experience, that from that day to this, I have never listened to nor told a dirty joke or story, and I never will."

Each of us has been asked to give his heart to our Lord and Savior. Speaking from the heavens while darkness covered the survivors of the great destruction on the western continent, Jesus, who had fulfilled the law of Moses, commanded the Nephites to offer a new sacrifice to him: "And ye shall offer up unto me no more the shedding of blood; yea, your sacrifices and your burnt offerings shall be done away, for I will accept none of your sacrifices and your burnt offerings. And ye shall offer for a sacrifice unto me a broken heart and a contrite spirit. And whoso cometh unto me with a broken heart and a contrite spirit, him will I baptize with fire and with the Holy Ghost. . . ." (3 Nephi 9:19-20.)

We are asked to give him a broken heart, a heart that is subdued, humbled, and tamed, and a contrite spirit, one that is humbled and repentant. President Harold B. Lee taught: "The righteous man . . . is humble and does not parade his righteousness to be seen of men. . . . The righteous man strives for self-improvement knowing that he has daily need of repentance for his misdeeds or his neglect." (*Stand Ye in Holy Places* [Deseret Book, 1974], pp. 332-33.)

"Behold, the Lord requireth the heart and a willing mind. . . ." (D&C 64:34.) Jesus himself is the epitome of one who has a humble or broken heart. This is illustrated so well in the following New Testament account:

> He riseth from supper, and laid aside his garments; and took a towel, and girded himself.
>
> After that he poureth water into a bason, and began to wash the disciples' feet, and to wipe them with the towel wherewith he was girded.
>
> So after he had washed their feet, and had taken his garments, and was set down again, he said unto them, Know ye what I have done to you?
>
> Ye call me Master and Lord: and ye say well; for so I am.
>
> If I then, your Lord and Master, have washed your feet; ye also ought to wash another's feet.
>
> For I have given you an example, that ye should do as I have done to you.
>
> Verily, verily, I say unto you, The servant is not greater than his lord; neither he that is sent greater than he that sent him.
>
> If ye know these things, happy are ye if ye do them. (John 13:4-5, 12-17.)

Jesus is the supreme example of what he has asked us to be.

Alma, speaking to his son, said: "Preach unto them repentance, and faith on the Lord Jesus Christ; teach them to humble themselves and to be meek and lowly in heart. . . . Teach them to never be weary of good works, but to be meek and lowly in heart; for such shall find rest to their souls." (Alma 37:33-34.)

We have been admonished to be humble—to have broken hearts and contrite spirits. We cannot save ourselves, and Jesus can save none except those who permit him. Those who are stubborn, arrogant, and self-sufficient cannot be saved. People who have these characteristics are called hardhearted by the Lord.

". . . he hath spoken unto you in a still small voice, but ye were past feeling, that ye could not feel his words. . . . O, then, why is it, that ye can be so hard in your hearts?" (1 Nephi 17:45-46.)

". . . he that will harden his heart, the same receiveth the lesser portion of the word; and he that will not harden his heart, to him is given the greater portion of the word. . . ." (Alma 12:10.)

The Savior always stands ready to help a person change his heart from hard, or unyielding, to broken, or subdued.

"For this people's heart is waxed gross, and their ears are dull of hearing, and their eyes they have closed; lest at any time they should see with their eyes, and hear with their ears, and should understand with their heart, and should be converted, and I should heal them." (Matthew 13:15.)

The Book of Mormon has excellent examples of people's hearts being changed from worldly things to those of the Lord. King Benjamin saw this great change in his people and said: ". . . he [the Lord] hath spiritually begotten you; for ye say that your hearts are changed. . . ." (Mosiah 5:7.)

Alma, speaking to his people, said, "Have ye

experienced this mighty change in your hearts?" (Alma 5:14.)

We learn from the Old Testament that God gave Saul "another heart." (1 Samuel 10:9.) If one has a hard, rebellious heart, it is because he is not utilizing the breastplate of righteousness. Unrighteousness produces a hard heart, while righteousness produces a broken heart, a tender heart, a humble, receptive heart, a pure heart.

In a heart protected by God's armor, there is a desire to do good. (Mosiah 5:2.) The Lord says: ". . . for I will go before your face. I will be on your right hand and on your left, and my Spirit shall be in your hearts. . . ." (D&C 84:88.)

The consequences of not having the armor in place were explained by Nephi: "For behold, at that day [our day] shall he [Satan] rage in the hearts of the children of men. . . ." (2 Nephi 28:20.)

What is in a person's heart determines what he speaks. ". . . out of the abundance of the heart the mouth speaketh. . . ." (Matthew 12:34.) What is in a person's heart determines his actions, his behavior, and what he is. "As [a man] thinketh in his heart, so is he." (Proverbs 23:7.) Therefore, we are told, "Let virtue garnish thy thoughts unceasingly." (D&C 121:45.) If we exercise the mental discipline to cast out all unwholesome, unworthy thoughts and let only uplifting, righteous, virtuous thoughts have place in our minds, we will become like our thoughts.

Some people seem to be spontaneously good, while others seem to be spontaneously evil. What we are is not something that is entirely of the mind—it flows also from the heart. The stream from the heart may be love, warmth, kindness, generosity, forgiveness, or it may be pettiness, jealousy, suspicion, hate, lust.

I remember witnessing an apparently spontaneous demonstration of unselfish love. I was studying at my desk in a classroom. The students had gone for the day.

After a while I got up, walked across the room, and paused to look out the window. It was spring, and in the vacant lot next door an elderly man in a wheelchair was spearing bits of paper with a long stick, putting the paper into his lap, then wheeling over to a bonfire and throwing the papers in. Nearby, his aged wife was busily raking weeds. As I watched, the old couple tried to move a large two-wheeled trailer. The tires of the trailer were sunken into the ground, and weeds were entwined in the spokes. The woman was pulling on the tongue and the man seated in his wheelchair was trying to move one of the wheels, but all of their efforts were to no avail. Seeing that they needed help, I went out and offered my services. Soon we were able to move the trailer to a space behind a garage. After the couple had thanked me, I remarked that it was certainly hard work cleaning the yard in the springtime. The man replied, "Oh, this isn't our yard. Our yard is over there," pointing to a small clean yard. "This yard belongs to our former neighbors," he continued. "They moved to another city a few months ago and rented their house to some young men. The renters moved out last week and left the yard looking like this—neglected and full of rubbish." He paused, then added, "We couldn't let our friends see their yard like this, so we are cleaning it up for them."

The couple worked diligently all week, and by Friday, the job was completed. As I watched from the classroom window, I saw the elderly man wheel over the rough ground in his neighbor's yard, make a torch on the end of a long pole, and burn off the final tufts of grass. I said, half aloud, "This is what it means to have a broken heart and contrite spirit. This is what it means to be a humble follower of Jesus Christ."

Recently a wonderful older brother in our ward appeared at our front door with a bushel of apples, which he had picked that day in his orchard. He said he thought we might enjoy them. I thanked him and

37

learned from our conversation that he and his wife had just returned from Sugar City, Idaho, where they had taken a truckload of apples for some of the victims of the Teton Dam flood disaster.

After he left and I had carried the apples to the storage room, I sat down and reflected. This man and his wife are not young, and there are limitations on their physical strength. How did they decide to not only give a truckload of apples to those in need, but also to travel hundreds of miles to deliver them? I determined that goodness must have flooded out of their hearts and into the mind, and the plan was formulated. Another person with a different kind of heart might have formulated a plan to get more from his apples than they were worth by putting the small apples in the bottom and the large ones on top.

Wouldn't it be nice if each of us were like the elderly man and woman who cleaned their neighbor's yard, or my friend with the apples? Goodness seems to flow from the heart that is protected by the breastplate of righteousness. If we permit unwholesome, unrighteous things into our hearts, they become hardened to things that are right and good. We therefore need to protect our hearts at all times with the breastplate of righteousness.

"Now the end of the commandment is charity out of a pure heart [pure: free from adulterants or impurities, not mixed, free from defilement], and of a good conscience, and of faith unfeigned." (1 Timothy 1:5.)

Without charity out of a pure heart, the kingdom of God could not have been established or continued.

Hannah Cornaby and her husband were converted to the gospel in England. They crossed the plains and their sacrifices continued in Utah. Brother Cornaby was called to leave Salt Lake City and go southward to Utah Lake to increase the meager food supply of the Saints by fishing. Hannah records the following incident, which occurred during the absence of her husband:

38

One morning having, as usual, attended to family prayer, in which, with greater significance than is often used, we asked, "Give us this day our daily bread," and having eaten a rather scanty breakfast—every morsel we had in the house—Edith was wondering what we should have for dinner, and why Pa did not send us some fish. I, too, was anxious, not having heard from Provo for some days; so telling my darlings I would go and see if Sister Ellen Jackson, (whose husband was also one of the fishing party,) had heard any news, I started off. Sister Jackson had not heard from the fishery; but was quite cheerful, and telling me how well her garden was growing, added that the radishes were fit for use, and insisted that I must have some. It was good to see something to eat; and, quite pleased, I bade her good morning. Passing on my way, the house of Brother Charles Gray, Sister Gray asked me where I had got such fine radishes. I told her, and offered to divide with her, to which she agreed, providing I would take in exchange some lettuce and cress, of which she had plenty. She filled a pan with these; and I hurried away thinking how pleased my children would be, if only we had bread to eat with them. As I was passing Brother Simon Baker's house, Sister Baker saw me and invited me in. I told her I had left my children, and could not stop. She then asked me where I had got such nice green stuff, and when I told her, and offered her some, she replied, "if I could exchange some for butter, she would be glad." She then gave me a nice piece of fresh butter, which had just come from their dairy on the Jordan, and also a large slice of cheese. If I only had bread, I thought, how good these would be! Just then my eyes rested upon a large vessel full of broken bread. Sister Baker, seeing I had noticed it, told me its history. It had been sent the day before, in a sack, to the canyon where her husband had a number of men working. On the way it had fallen from the wagon, and been crushed under the wheel. She did not know what to do with it, remarking that she would offer me some of it but feared I would feel insulted, although assuring me it was perfectly clean. I accepted her offer, when, filling a large pan, she sent her daughter home with me to carry it.

The children were watching for my return; and when they saw the bread, they clapped their hands with delight. Bread, butter, cheese, radishes, lettuce, and cress! What a dinner we had that day! Elijah never enjoyed the dinner the ravens brought him more than I did that meal; nor more fully understood that a kind Providence had furnished it. (Hannah Cornaby, *Autobiography and Poems*, 1881, pp. 41-42.)

How wonderfully pleasant even difficult times can be when one wears the breastplate of righteousness as

Hannah Cornaby did! And one is twice blessed, as Hannah was, if he has the opportunity of associating with those who also wear the breastplate of righteousness.

The Prophet Joseph Smith wore the breastplate of righteousness throughout his lifetime. He remained humble, tenderhearted, submissive—in a word, pure. Consider his greatness of heart as you read the following letter, which he wrote to members of the Quorum of the Twelve while they were laboring as missionaries in England:

"How pleasing it is for the brethren to dwell together in unity! " Let the Saints of the Most High ever cultivate this principle, and the most glorious blessings must result, not only to them individually, but to the whole Church. . . .

There are many things of much importance, on which you ask counsel, but which I think you will be perfectly able to decide upon, as you are more conversant with the peculiar circumstances than I am; and I feel great confidence in your united wisdom; therefore you will excuse me for not entering into detail. If I should see anything that is wrong, I would take the privilege of making known my mind to you, and pointing out the evil. . . .

Beloved brethren, you must be aware in some measure of my feelings, when I contemplate the great work which is now rolling on, and the relationship which I sustain to it, while it is extending to distant lands, and thousands are embracing it. I realize in some measure my responsibility, and the need I have of support from above, and wisdom from on high, that I may be able to teach this people, which have now become a great people, the principles of righteousness, and lead them agreeably to the will of Heaven; so that they may be perfected, and prepared to meet the Lord Jesus Christ when He shall appear in great glory. Can I rely on your prayers to our heavenly Father on my behalf, and on all the prayers of all my brethren and sisters in England, (whom having not seen, yet I love), that I may be enabled to escape every stratagem of Satan, surmount every difficulty, and bring this people to the enjoyment of those blessings which are reserved for the righteous? I ask this at your hands in the name of the Lord Jesus Christ.

In conclusion the Prophet said:

. . . Let every selfish feeling be not only buried, but annihilated; and let love to God and man predominate. . . . Give my kind love to all the brethren and sisters, and tell them I should have been pleased to come over to England to see them, but I am afraid that I shall be under necessity of remaining here for some time; therefore I give them a pressing invitation to come and see me.

I remain, dear brethren, yours affectionately, Joseph Smith. (*History of the Church* 4:226-32.)

We are admonished again and again by the Lord, through his prophet, to be of one heart. We can never be of one heart with the Lord and with the prophet unless our hearts are pure. And our hearts can be pure if we each wear the breastplate of righteousness.

Chapter 5

PREPARATION OF THE GOSPEL OF PEACE

*Your feet shod with the preparation
of the gospel of peace, which I have sent mine
angels to commit unto you. (D&C 27:16.)
And your feet shod with the preparation of the
gospel of peace. (Ephesians 6:15.)*

The Lord chose the shoes or battle boots as being representative of preparation in the gospel of peace. Roman battle boots were sandals that laced high around the calves of the legs, and had soles thick enough to protect the feet. Sturdy but open so the feet could get air, they permitted maximum mobility.

To understand the importance of preparation let's picture a soldier in battle, beautifully arrayed with an impressive helmet, a magnificent breastplate, protective armor about the loins, a large, beautifully decorated shield, and a sword that glistens in the sun, but minus the least notable and perhaps the least impressive part of the battle gear, the shoes. Take off the shoes, take them away, and if the soldier, who is bearing the weight of the heavy armor, takes a few steps in any direction his bare feet are cut and bruised by sharp rocks, or injured by burning sand, or thorns. Helpless, he surrenders or is quickly overcome by the enemy.

Preparation in the gospel of peace may be compared with putting on the battle boots. A soldier of the Lord Jesus Christ must be prepared and have peace inside to successfully wage war against evil.

The leaders of the Roman army constantly emphasized preparation. They were convinced and proved to the world that drill and discipline were vital to the success of the army.

> Vegetius unceasingly emphasized the importance of constant drill and severe discipline. . . . "Victory in war," he states in his opening sentence, "does not depend entirely upon number or mere courage; only skill and discipline will insure it." Vegetius' work is filled with maxims that have become familiar in our time. . . . "Few men are born brave; many become so through training and force of discipline." . . . A soldier, thus perfected in his art, so far from showing any backwardness to engage, will be eager for an opportunity of distinguishing himself. (Thomas R. Phillips, ed., *The Military Institutions of the Romans* [Harrisburg, Pa.: The Military Service Publishing Co., 1944], pp. 9, 15.)

Preparation is most often not very glamorous and usually does not bring immediate attention or immediate rewards, but it is vital.

Our feet are to be shod with the preparation of the gospel of peace, are to be on the strait and narrow path, eagerly advancing in the right direction.

Prior to his departure from this earth, our Savior said: "Peace I leave with you, my peace I give unto you: not as the world giveth, give I unto you. Let not your heart be troubled, neither let it be afraid." (John 14:27.)

Jesus could leave his peace with his disciples because through diligent effort they were prepared to receive it. He could not leave his peace with those who were unprepared.

Jesus had carefully instructed his disciples that they resided in the world, but they were not a part of the world. "If ye were of the world the world would love his own: but because ye are not of the world, but I have chosen you out of the world, therefore the world hateth you." (John 15:19.) He tells of conditions that are to precede his coming: "And in that day shall be heard of wars and rumors of wars, and the whole earth shall be in commotion, and men's hearts shall fail them, . . . And the love of men shall wax cold, and iniquity shall abound." (D&C 45:26-27.)

The true follower of the Lord Jesus Christ will be prepared and will be armed with the preparation of the gospel of peace. He who is truly prepared can act calmly in a crisis or in a critical situation. The following will illustrate this principle.

A person who is ill prepared might come upon an accident scene and begin weeping, wringing his hands, and possibly fainting, all of which would add to the confusion and the problem. In the same situation, one who is prepared would probably step forward with certainty, inspire trust and confidence in the victim and all others, utilize the principles he had previously learned, administer the necessary first aid, and be a major part of the solution. Such a person would have no fear or feeling of panic. Concern, yes; compassion, yes; but his previous industriousness and preparation would permit him to be of great service.

Why couldn't the first person act with the same calmness and efficiency? Because he is unprepared and thus is powerless to act. Lack of preparation brings frustration, anxiety, and fear; it not only renders a person powerless and useless, but even worse, he is often a detriment in a stressful situation. It would be better if he were not to appear at the scene, because he would probably raise the anxiety level of many others.

The Lord has said, "If ye are prepared ye shall not fear." (D&C 38:30.) He wants the best for all of his children. We are blessed with free agency and we must seize the initiative. We must learn to act and not to be acted upon. "And the Messiah cometh in the fulness of time, that he may redeem the children of men from the fall. And because that they are redeemed from the fall they have become free forever, knowing good from evil; to act for themselves and not to be acted upon, save it be by the punishment of the law at the great and last day, according to the commandments which God hath given." (2 Nephi 2:26.)

The Lord honors us, his children, by the trust and confidence he places in us to exercise our free agency. Since childhood I have been impressed with the story of David, the shepherd boy. His father asked him to go on an errand, saying, in essence, "I would like you to take food to your brothers in the Israelite army." David approached the Israelites as they were pitched in battle against the Philistines. There he saw the giant Goliath, a representative of the Philistines, who was shouting out threats and intimidating the whole Israelite army.

David was astonished that no one would respond to the challenge. Approaching one of his older brothers, he asked, "Is there not a cause?" Then he volunteered to go out as the champion of the Israelites, and King Saul accepted his offer.

David selected five smooth stones to use in his sling. As he crossed the field with a staff in his hand, Goliath gave a tremendous roar, crying out, "Am I a dog, that thou comest to me with staves?" David replied, "Thou comest to me with a sword, and with a spear, and with a shield: but I come to thee in the name of the Lord of hosts, the God of the armies of Israel, whom thou hast defied." The first stone found its mark, and Goliath fell. David then destroyed Goliath with his own sword, thus freeing Israel from the oppression of the Philistines. The Philistines fled and many lives were saved because one young man, David, said, "Is there not a cause?" Then, with the strength of God, he went out to defend his people. (1 Samuel 17.)

I have returned again and again to this powerful story. I find no place where David's father commanded him to go down and save Israel by defeating the Philistines. I see no place where Saul asked him to be the champion of the Israelites. David saw the situation, he was prepared, and he had unwavering faith in the God of Israel. He didn't need to be asked or commanded. He chose; he took the initiative and made the decision, and with the Lord's help he freed his people from the oppression of the enemy.

Preparation brings excitement and a relish for the necessary conflict. A lack of preparation at best brings a lack of enthusiasm, and at worst, outright cowardice. Think for a moment of the well-prepared missionary and contrast him with the ill-prepared one. Or consider the well-prepared young woman in her new role as a wife and contrast her with the woman who is unprepared. Much, if not most, disappointment, disillusionment, frustration, and fear can be avoided by proper, persistent preparation.

In our day the Lord has said:

> For behold, it is not meet that I should command in all things; for he that is compelled in all things, the same is a slothful and not a wise servant; wherefore he receiveth no reward.
>
> Verily I say, men should be anxiously engaged in a good cause, and do many things of their own free will, and bring to pass much righteousness;
>
> For the power is in them, wherein they are agents unto themselves. And inasmuch as men do good they shall in nowise lose their reward.
>
> But he that doeth not anything until he is commanded, and receiveth a commandment with doubtful heart, and keepeth it with slothfulness, the same is damned. (D&C 58:26-29.)

The gospel is needed as much by the young as it is by the old. There is no one period of a person's life when it is more important to live the gospel than another. Each day well spent by an eight-year-old is preparation for the very next day, each succeeding day, and for the entire future. Each well-spent day is preparation for an eighty-year-old as well, and for his entire future. For the eighty-year-old, perhaps a succeeding day might soon be that very important first day in paradise; that day is worth preparing for, because if one is not prepared, that first day may be in spirit prison and not in paradise. Satan tries to destroy us spiritually with such thoughts as these: Later, when I grow up, I'll get serious about the gospel—maybe when I go on a mission; or, I'll repent in the future for marriage in the temple; or, I'll do it when we have children; or, when I have more time I'll do it.

We do not wait to prepare in the future. We prepare now. We are in eternity, and there is no beginning or end. The key to preparation is found in section 11 of the Doctrine and Covenants, in a revelation to Hyrum Smith through the Prophet Joseph. One word reappears throughout the section: *desire*. Desire, or a derivation of it, appears in verses 3, 8, 10, 14, 17, 21, and 27. For example:

"Verily, verily I say unto you, even as you desire of me so it shall be done unto you; and, if you desire, you shall be the means of doing much good in this generation." (D&C 11:8.)

"And then, behold, according to your desires, yea, even according to your faith shall it be done unto you." (D&C 11:17.)

If Hyrum desires a part in the Lord's great latter-day work, he is told, he may have it, but he must prepare. He is told to keep the Lord's commandments, hold his peace, appeal to the Lord's Spirit, and cleave unto the Lord with all his heart. He is further instructed: "Behold, this is your work, to keep my commandments, yea, with all your might, mind, and strength. Seek not to declare my word, but first seek to obtain my word, and then shall your tongue be loosed; then, if you desire, you shall have my Spirit and my word, yea, the power of God unto the convincing of men."

It is exciting to learn that in this section, the Lord is not only promising great opportunities to Hyrum Smith, but the promise is extended to all of us if we have good desires. "Behold, I speak unto all who have good desires, and have thrust in their sickle to reap." (D&C 11:27.)

One's entire life to a particular point in time becomes part of the next decision to be made. A person who has smoked a pack of cigarettes each day for twenty years, if offered a cigarette, will almost certainly accept it and smoke it. Conversely, a person who has never smoked will undoubtedly turn the offer down.

Joseph Fielding Smith was a faithful, obedient, scholarly apostle for more than half a century before he became president of the Church. During his administration he probably didn't surprise anyone. All expected him to be diligent, true, and faithful, and he was.

The Lord has counseled us to be anxiously engaged in a good cause and seek to bring to pass much righteousness of our own free will. As we get into decision-making situations, if we know the truth, have lived by truth, and have made right decisions, it is natural for us to continue to make right decisions. Some have arrived at such a condition of obedience to truth and right and have become so totally dependable that the Lord has entrusted them with great power. Consider Enoch; Nephi, the son of Helaman; Elijah; and many others.

Much of the victory may be secured before one enters the arena where a particular battle takes place. We must prepare in the gospel of peace. Peace can come only when conflict has ceased inside. An individual can have complete peace inside only when he becomes totally committed to all aspects of the gospel. If he is still struggling and trying to determine if he will commit himself fully, he has less energy for the conflict. It would be devastating if a soldier went into battle wondering if he should even be there. When peace is inside, the individual can excel in the external conflict.

The scriptures teach us to have an eye single to the glory of God. (D&C 4:5.) Otherwise we may not have the capacity to withstand the heat of the battle, and might bolt and run.

We prepare for future service and future conflicts by studying the scriptures, listening to the words of our inspired leaders, and applying all of these true teachings

49

and principles in our daily lives. We prepare for the future by living the way the Lord wants us to live. If we let time work in our favor in the present, there is assurance that it will work in our favor in the future. Paul wrote: "Be not deceived; God is not mocked: for whatsoever a man soweth, that shall he also reap." (Galatians 6:7.)

A number of years ago our family had the privilege of becoming acquainted with the Dennis Flake family of Boise, Idaho, a marvelous family consisting of the parents and ten children. At that time the two oldest children, sons, went into the mission field.

About seventeen years passed by, and again I was in their home. The Flakes had always worked hard for the necessities of life, but there were few luxuries. Brother Flake, a former member of the stake presidency, shared with me his experience of being called and ordained a patriarch. His wife helped him by typing the blessings. He expressed gratitude to the Lord for the blessings he and his companion had in being able to associate with and contribute to the youth of their stake in this manner.

Sister Flake said, "But there is one thing I feel badly about. Our last son is in the mission field [five had served and returned], and right now, just as President Kimball is stressing missionary work, we have run out of missionary sons."

President Flake looked at his wife, smiled, and quietly replied, "Yes, but we have twenty grandsons."

I sat and marveled at the blessings the Lord had poured out upon the Flake family in the intervening years. I had a mental image of the windows of heaven being opened and blessings poured down in such abundance that they could hardly be contained. This fine couple had planted in their childhood, youth, and adult years. They had planted when hard work, sacrifice, and pain were called for, but they had planted joyfully. And now the harvest—how fruitful, how abundant, how delicious it was for the Lord, for the Church, for themselves, for their children, and for many, many others. They could have been lazy, slothful, selfish, or greedy. But they had prepared well, and the blessings of today are the result of previous diligent, faithful moments.

One cannot procrastinate planting indefinitely, for there comes a time when the time to plant has passed. By then, others who have planted will be enjoying the fruits of their labors and experiencing more fullness than ever before, while those who have not prepared, who have not planted, will be left with emptiness, barrenness, disappointment. (See D&C 45:2.) They will know of their emptiness because they will experience it, but they can have no comprehension of the fullness they are missing, for that can only be experienced and enjoyed by those who have earned the harvest. Therein lies the greatness of the tragedy.

The choices we make are often crucial in terms of their consequences. The Lord is ever anxious to bless us and help us, but we must decide whether or not we will permit him to do so. In the scriptures we see clearly the consequences of man's choices—choices that led some to share with their fellowmen and build the kingdom of God; choices that led some to selfishness and pride and to tear down the kingdom of God; choices that permitted some to behold Jesus Christ and live in a time of happiness and righteousness; choices that led some to stone the prophets and be destroyed from the face of the earth because of extreme wickedness. The choices remain before us today. We can be greedy and vile or generous and righteous. We can prepare to dwell with the Lord in happiness or we can suffer for our sins.

The Book of Mormon leaves no question as to individual moral agency. Following are some of the explicit verses:

"Therefore, cheer up your hearts, and remember that ye are free to act for yourselves—to choose the way of everlasting death or the way of eternal life." (2 Nephi 10:23.)

"Wherefore, the Lord God gave unto man that he

should act for himself. Wherefore, man could not act for himself save it should be that he was enticed by the one or the other." (2 Nephi 2:16.)

Making right choices in the present leads to other right choices in the future. Hence, making right decisions becomes the best preparation for future right decisions.

Our feet must be shod with the preparation of the gospel of peace. Peace must begin inside individuals; it cannot come to the world unless it starts inside righteous people. Those who have such peace individually can then collectively radiate and influence peace throughout the world.

Chapter 6

THE SHIELD
OF FAITH

Taking the shield of faith wherewith
ye shall be able to quench all the fiery darts of
the wicked. (D&C 27:17.)

Paul admonished the Ephesians: "Above all, taking the shield of faith, wherewith ye shall be able to quench all the fiery darts of the wicked." (Ephesians 6:16.) In the Doctrine and Covenants account (D&C 27:17) the words "above all" are not included. The new English Bible (p. 335) reads, "and with all these take the great shield of faith. . . ."

The meaning is clear. The shield is not meant to be the only armament we have; it is to be used in conjunction with all of the rest of the armor. A soldier without a sword, a helmet, and other proper equipment could not last long in the battle without being wounded.

The Roman shield spoken of by Paul was a large body shield four feet long and two and a half feet wide, curved at the top and bottom and slightly curved on each side. It was made of thin sheets of wood glued together so that the grain of each piece was at right angles with the next piece. The edges were bound with wrought iron or bronze, while the outside surface was covered with leather. It was decorated, and each emblem was a different color to aid recognition in battle. Each soldier also had his name and century (one hundred men) written on his shield. (*The Roman Imperial Army of the First and Second Centuries A.D.* [New York: Funk and Wagnalls, 1969], pp. 128-29.)

As the soldiers advanced into battle, often they were met with a barrage of enemy arrows (referred to as fiery darts). Some had been dipped in pitch, lighted, and then shot from the archer's bow. A well-trained, alert soldier protected himself from the flaming arrows by quickly putting his shield in front of him. Obviously the shield was his chief defensive weapon. In close combat it was used to fend off the blows of the enemy. It was also used as an offensive weapon. As a soldier attacked, he would thrust his shield forward or lunge forward to throw the enemy off balance and gain an advantage.

"A trained legionary knows how to fend and lunge with his shield with marvelous agility, and by means of the solid metal base in the center he can strike a tremendous blow," wrote William Stearns Davis. (*A Day in Old Rome* [New York: Bible and Tannen, 1961], p. 318.)

How appropriate that faith is the spiritual shield that is a vital part of our armor. The shield of faith is the part of the armor that is out in front, pushing forward, quenching the flaming arrows of the wicked so they do not wound us or destroy us spiritually.

A soldier without a shield would be in grave danger. A person without the spiritual shield of faith would also be in grave danger.

The first principle of the gospel is not faith alone, but faith in the Lord Jesus Christ. That makes a lot of difference. For some, the concept of faith is abstract and difficult to understand. But faith in the Lord Jesus Christ is not abstract; it is concrete and understandable. Knowing that the first principle of the gospel is faith in the Lord Jesus Christ makes it much easier to know what path to follow to increase our faith. If we are going to increase our faith in Jesus Christ, we must first increase our knowledge of him.

Many of us have mentally followed the Savior's steps through his earthly ministry, so we know of his love and goodness. We have visualized the touching scene in Jericho when the Master paused beneath a sycamore tree, invited a despised tax collector to come down, and informed him that he would abide with him that day. This act would not add to our Lord's popularity, but he had not come to the earth to be popular— he had come to save men's souls.

After a short time with the Savior, the greedy and dishonest tax collector Zacchaeus said: "Behold, Lord, the half of my goods I give to the poor; and if I have taken any thing from any man by false accusation, I restore him fourfold." (Luke 19:8.)

The tax collector then became generous through the example, love, and teachings of the Master.

In another example of the Savior's love, a woman taken in the act of adultery was humiliated by the self-righteous persons who loudly proclaimed her sins. She was brought before the Savior, who stooped down and wrote with his finger on the ground, then said, "He that is without sin among you, let him first cast a stone at her." He again wrote on the ground, then raised up and said, "Woman, where are these thine accusers? hath no man condemned thee?" She replied, "No man, Lord." And Jesus said to her, "Neither do I condemn thee: go, and sin no more." (John 8:3-11.)

As Saul traveled on the road to Damascus, "breathing out threatenings" against the saints, a bright light appeared and the Savior spoke. "Saul, Saul, why persecutest thou me? And he said, Who art thou, Lord? And the Lord said, I am Jesus whom thou persecutest: It is hard for thee to kick against the pricks." (Acts 9:4-5.) The Savior was most concerned about Saul's well-being.

We are deeply indebted to God for sending his Son and for the example the Son set for us. We should each resolve to study his life. If we are truly honest in heart and desire to have more faith in him, we will increase our knowledge of him and be obedient to his teachings. James said, "Faith without works is dead." (James 2:20.) We could say also that faith without works isn't faith—hope, maybe; belief, perhaps; but not faith. Faith includes physical, spiritual, and intellectual effort.

The perfect Son of God came to the earth to save us. It is in him that we have life. There is no other name whereby we can be saved.

Repeatedly in our sacred scriptures, especially in the Doctrine and Covenants, our Lord admonishes us to endure. It is only in faith that we can endure. "And we know that all men must repent and believe on the name of Jesus Christ, and worship the Father in his name, and endure in faith on his name to the end, or they cannot be saved in the kingdom of God." (D&C 20:29.) We read further, "He that endureth in faith and doeth my will, the same shall overcome, and shall receive an inheritance upon the earth. . . ." (D&C 63:20.)

Endure means to carry on, despite hardships. It also means to suffer patiently without yielding. Enduring is necessary because each of us encounters great opposition. This is expressly taught by the prophet Lehi: "For it must needs be, that there is an opposition in all things. If not so, my first-born in the wilderness, righteousness could not be brought to pass, neither wickedness, neither good nor bad. . . ." (2 Nephi 2:11.)

Often it is not the overwhelming, frightening, or difficult events in life that turn one out of the pathway to eternal life; rather, it is nagging little things that wear a person down and cause him to give up short of the goal.

This was well illustrated in a story told by Elder James A. Cullimore of the First Quorum of the Seventy:

An interesting experience is related by Mr. Harleigh M. Rosenberger: "Several years ago a man was being interviewed on a radio. He had started to walk across the United States on foot, from California to New York. He had reached a point halfway across. Reporters asked him about his experience. Finally, the question came, 'Sir, what would you say has been your most difficult experience so far?'

"The traveler thought long. Through his mind went the toilsome climb over mountain passes; hot dry stretches of desert. Sun. Wind. Then he said quietly, 'I guess my greatest problem was that the sand kept getting into my shoes.'

"So that was it. The sand in his shoes. Not some great crisis that he had faced. Not some danger that had almost taken his life. But sand; sand that wore blisters on the soles of his feet. Sand that ground its way between the pores of his skin and irritated constantly, that made every step an agony. Sand in his shoes."

Life is like that. It is not always the great crisis in life that crushes. Not always the deepest sorrows or the great disappointments. Most often, it is the constant irritation of small things— things insignificant in themselves. We can stand up to the big things of life. But the petty things can often cause our downfall, until we say ofttimes it is just one thing after another. For the little things have a way of wearing down our inner reserves of strength. (*BYU Speeches of the Year*, May 2, 1967, pp. 5-6.)

It is not unusual or uncommon to hear words such as these: "It isn't fair; it just isn't fair." "Why did it have to happen to me?" "Why us?" "Why did the Lord let this happen?" "I just don't know if I can go on." Such questions or statements are often uttered in pain, in sorrow, in despair, and sometimes in bitterness.

If we stop and reflect, we really do know more than perhaps we are remembering at that particular moment. We know, for example, where we lived before we came here. We know of the circumstances when our Heavenly Father's plan was presented by the Savior, and we know the reaction of Lucifer, the son of the morning. Some persons were confused and supported the usurper. Those who were thoughtful, faithful, and courageous supported the Lord's plan. Note the word *plan*. A plan is defined as "any detailed program or method worked out beforehand for the accomplishment of an objective, a goal." In the Book of Abraham we read:

And there stood one among them that was like unto God, and he said unto those who were with him: We will go down, for there is space there, and we will take of these materials, and we will make an earth whereon these may dwell;

And we will prove them herewith, to see if they will do all things whatsoever the Lord their God shall command them;

And they who keep their first estate shall be added upon; and they who keep not their first estate shall not have glory in the same kingdom with those who keep their first estate; and they who keep their second estate shall have glory added upon their heads for ever and ever. (Abraham 3:24-26.)

A plan, a method, a program was presented and joyfully accepted by us, a plan by which we could progress and become like our Father in heaven. The great genius of the plan, I believe, is that the omnipotent God, Jesus Christ, would condescend to personally come down to the earth and be our Savior, our exemplar, so that we could see his greatness in mortality.

We want to be like the Savior. It is difficult to resist the love and the beckoning hand of him who not only says he loves us, but who also demonstrated it and continues to demonstrate it in a most amazing way.

His plan, if accepted and adopted by all of us, would lead us triumphant over all evil back to the bosom of our Father in heaven.

Let's accept the plan of salvation. Let's accept the rules. The rules include an adversary, opportunities, and testing. Let's quit fighting against the rules. Those who understand the game and its rules and live by them are good sports. A good sport is defined as "a person known for the manner of his acceptance of the rules of a game or of a difficult situation." The opposite is a poor sport, one who is "lacking in mental or moral quality, inferior, inadequate, lacking in value."

If we spend all our time questioning the very rules, the very plan, the very program that we accepted in our pre-earth life, we will waste a lot of time and expend much effort in vain. The plan is in existence; it was adopted by us. It is right. It can bring us total joy and success.

Can you imagine how frustrating a basketball game would be if someone kept asking why the ball is the size it is, why the basket is ten feet high, why it can't be lowered, and why we can't have more players and more rest periods? When previously established rules are accepted, there is excitement and accomplishment in a game. So it is with life. When we exercise faith in God and accept his plan once and for all, when we select his way, we take a great step forward toward returning to his presence and obtaining eternal life and the joys and opportunities that accompany it.

Our shield that makes it possible for us to endure joyfully is our faith in the Lord Jesus Christ. When the challenges, trials, and difficulties come, the first thing a Latter-day Saint does is put his trust, his confidence, and his faith in the Lord Jesus Christ, the Holy One of Israel, our Savior.

Certainly one needs the faith to endure, to endure disappointment, heartache, illness, pain, and suffering. It takes faith not to give in when others would become faint-hearted and surrender, or, if not surrender, at least complain bitterly about the circumstances they are in and the conditions that surround them.

There are some, however, who do not just hold on in such a situation, some who boldly thrust their shield of faith forward and charge; and with God's help the circumstances are changed.

When President David O. McKay was eight years old, his father, David McKay, received a mission call. Because President McKay's mother, Jennette, was expecting a baby, his father was reluctant to accept the call. When Jennette read the letter from the President of the Church, however, she was decisive. "Of course you must accept," she said; "you need not worry about me. David O. and I will manage things nicely!" David

McKay left for Scotland just a few days before a baby girl was born. Sister McKay did not merely survive in her husband's absence; she worked so hard and managed so well that there was enough money to have a long-hoped-for addition added to their home. She did not tell her husband; it was her surprise. On the day David McKay returned, the family sat listening to his experiences, and one of his children asked if he had seen any miracles. He put his arm around his wife and replied, "Your mother is the greatest miracle that one could ever find!" (Llewelyn R. McKay, *Home Memories of President David O. McKay* [Deseret Book, 1956], pp. 5-6.) David and Jennette Evans McKay each had the shield of faith and knew how to use it. Because of them, many have been blessed.

Without the shield against the adversary and his wicked hosts, seen and unseen, we would be worn down and give up. Martin Harris always declared he didn't leave the Church, the Church left him. While the Saints endured the hardships of the move to Missouri, Illinois, and the West, he remained in Kirtland, Ohio. He had dropped his shield of faith, had become faint-hearted, and had remained behind, separated from the fulness of the gospel and from the advancing kingdom of God. In his sunset years he lamented his error, but the years of joyfully contributing to God's work were gone and could not be called back. They were gone, as was the magnificent contribution he could have made.

Whittier concludes his poem "Maud Muller" with the words, "Of all sad words of tongue or pen, the saddest are these: 'It might have been.'" It "might have been" for Martin Harris if he had held the shield of faith before him and deflected all the potentially hurtful arrows of persecution, pride, envy, suspicion, and self-pity that separated him from his place in God's kingdom for such a long time.

This life is a preparation for another existence, for opportunities beyond our present comprehension. Each of us is a child of God; each of us has tests, though for each the tests differ. We may be tested according to our needs. The test for a shy, retiring person may be a mission call or a call to a leadership position. One such as he would perhaps rather work in the background and support someone else in the spotlight, but our loving Lord desires that we each develop courage and self-confidence and become more capable and effective. Another person may have much self-confidence and feel comfortable in the spotlight and desire to be there, and for him, it might well be a test to be out of the spotlight.

If we need lessons of meekness and humility, if we need the broken heart and the contrite spirit, Heavenly Father will give us the opportunities to develop these qualities. Some have not been able to stand the test of being thrust into the limelight, while others have not measured up to the demands of being out of the spotlight.

Martin Harris, James J. Strang, Sidney Rigdon, and others in the early days of the Church wanted more recognition and failed the test when the spotlight pointed another direction. Such men as Joseph Smith, Brigham Young, and Heber C. Kimball, by contrast, acquired the great qualities needed whether in or out of the spotlight.

Our all-wise, all-knowing Father in heaven is interested in what is most important for each of his children. He wants each of us to make a maximum contribution, but above all, he wants each of us to return to him when our journey is concluded.

Many who have left this world with little recognition have lived remarkable lives. Many mothers have lived most noble lives out of the spotlight and have emulated the most noble of virtues and helped their children to learn them. They have permitted recognition to largely pass by because in the eternal scheme of things it was right to do so. A person needs to take the shield of faith when he is doing God's will in order to be protected against the sophisticated reasoning and snide remarks of the unknowing who may see simple virtues as valueless. We do not perceive all the eternal lessons we need to learn in this life, but our loving Heavenly Father does.

One is not finally judged by well-publicized or acclaimed contributions, but by how well he has performed his particular mission. While our discernment may be faulty, the Lord's never is. If we will commit ourselves to him and strive to serve him with all our heart, might, mind, and strength, he will direct us to do that which eternally will be for our best good, for the best good of our fellow beings, and for the best good of his glorious work. If it so happens that some in this world acclaim our contributions, that is fine. If they do not, that's also fine. For we serve a Master not known to the world, and we work to build a kingdom that is not accepted by the world.

Faith in the Lord Jesus Christ is not a mystery. By learning more of him and doing his will, we can put ourselves in a position where he can bestow the gift of faith upon us, and as we exercise faith, he blesses us. We do not have to live out our lives wondering if what we are doing is right; the fruits or rewards come as we exercise faith. These evidences encourage us to exercise faith again in some other aspect of life, and as we receive results—such as experiencing the companionship of the Holy Ghost, feeling happiness, becoming more sensitive, increasing our understanding—our faith is increased just that much more, until we are able to accomplish truly remarkable things.

Faith in the Lord Jesus Christ can accomplish great things in our lives. Hope can replace doubt. Happiness can replace unhappiness. Righteousness can replace sin. Love can replace hate. Faith in the Lord Jesus Christ is the first principle of the gospel and probably the most discussed principle in the Church. But perhaps it is also the most under-used principle.

The shield of faith must be held alertly and used skillfully every day of our lives. Never can we lay it aside even for a moment. It is to be carried by every son and daughter of God, for each is precious in the Lord's eyes.

It is not just church leaders and missionaries who must have and use the shield of faith expertly. True, some are positioned on the battlefield where the battle may be raging, and where they are fighting for their spiritual lives and for the spiritual lives of others. Others may be in more remote positions, and, unless they observe carefully, they might think that the enemy is not present and that there is no need to carry the shield on the arm and hold it watchfully. They may complacently think they can rest for a short period or perhaps lay the shield down for a little season, placing it nearby where it could be quickly secured and placed in position.

Such reasoning is deadly, for the enemy is the master of the silent, swift attack. In fact, many have been attacked and spiritually wounded even though they have declared vehemently that no enemy appeared and that there was no attack. Some near spiritual death have not been able to discern the seriousness of the wound, and with their last breath have declared that some who stood near them who are completely whole were really the wounded ones. This is the cunning of the evil one, the archenemy of God, the master deceiver who may attack quickly, wound fatally, and persuade his victim that there has never been a battle and that he, the victim, has not received a scratch.

Others may set the armor aside and permit it to gather dust and become corroded with disuse. The cunning enemy inflicts a superficial wound, then another, over a long period of time. Such persons can become immobilized and completely incapacitated without even realizing it. The tragedy is that they are always looking toward the horizon for a sign of the impending attack, wondering and hoping that they will have the skill and courage to survive the one big attack, the one great temptation, the one expected monumental trial in life. The enemy whom they have looked for on the horizon has, in reality, been in camp for a long time, disguised, unrecognized, working systematically, imperceptibly, accepted by the ignorant, the slothful, those who did not know how to watch and protect themselves from destruction.

Yes, it takes effort, energy, concentration, diligence, and just plain hard work to keep the shield firmly in place, but the alternative is too terrible to experiment with. It is entirely possible that the first experiment may be the last experiment. The blows may be fatal. If not, there may be a painful, extended recovery period that will require much more effort than the initial bearing up of the shield. Therefore, we must take up the shield of faith wherewith we will be able to quench all the fiery darts of the wicked.

Chapter 7

THE HELMET
OF SALVATION

And take the helmet of salvation.
(D&C 27:18; Ephesians 6:17.)

In 1837 the Prophet Joseph Smith was sitting next to Heber C. Kimball in the Kirtland Temple. He turned to Heber and said, "Brother Heber, the Spirit of the Lord has whispered to me: 'Let thy servant Heber go to England and proclaim my Gospel, and open the door of salvation to that nation. . . .' " (Whitney, *The Life of Heber C. Kimball*, p. 104.)

This would be the first mission across an ocean. The call came at a time when, according to John Taylor, many were passing "under a dark cloud." (B. H. Roberts, *The Life of John Taylor* [Bookcraft, 1963], p. 40.) Apostasy was rampant; the lives of the faithful were being threatened.

A member of the Twelve who was in a condition of apostasy told Heber he was a fool for accepting the call. Brigham Young said he did not feel that way, and prophesied that if Heber went, he would be prospered in the work and would have cause to rejoice. Heber spent several days in the Kirtland Temple praying and pleading with God to make him equal to the task. Robert Thompson describes the scene he beheld when he called for Elder Kimball to leave on his mission:

The day appointed for the departure of the Elders to England having arrived, I stepped into the house of Brother Kimball to ascertain when he would start; as I expected to accompany him two or three hundred miles, intending to spend my labors in Canada that season.

The door being partly open, I entered and felt struck with the sight which presented itself to my view. I would have retired, thinking that I was intruding, but I felt riveted to the spot. The father was pouring out his soul to that God "who rules on high," that he would grant him a prosperous voyage across the mighty ocean, and make him useful wherever his lot should be cast, and that He who "careth for sparrows, and feedeth the young ravens when they cry" would supply the wants of his wife and little ones in his absence. He then, like the patriarchs, and by virtue of his office, laid his hands upon their heads individually, leaving a father's blessing upon them, and commending them to the care and protection of God, while he should be engaged in preaching the Gospel in a foreign land. While thus engaged his voice was almost lost in the sobs of those around, who tried in vain to suppress them. The idea of being separated from their protector and father for so long a time was indeed painful. He proceeded, but his heart was too much affected to do so regularly. His emotions were great, and he was obliged to stop at intervals, while the big tears rolled down his cheeks, an index to the feelings which reigned in his bosom. My heart was not stout enough to refrain; in spite of myself I wept, and mingled my tears with theirs. At the same time I felt thankful that I had the privilege of contemplating such a scene. I realized that nothing could induce that man to tear himself from so affectionate a family group, from his partner and children who were so dear to him—nothing but a sense of duty and love to God and attachment to His cause. (*The Life of Heber C. Kimball*, pp. 108-9.)

Heber was in England eight months before the Prophet Joseph wrote to him and asked him to return, and he converted nearly 1500 persons in that short period. During his absence, Joseph Smith, Brigham Young, and other faithful Church leaders had to flee Kirtland to save their lives.

This historical incident, the beginning of missionary

work in England, is a superb example of acting and not being acted upon.

When hatred and other wickedness would have forced the Church and its leaders to take the defensive, bold action by the Lord through his Prophet ultimately brought thousands of converts and great strength to the Church.

The mission of the Church and of its members has always been clear. The Lord has told us, in modern revelation: "The field is white already to harvest." (D&C 4:4.) "Remember the worth of souls is great in the sight of God." (D&C 18:10.) "And if it so be that you should labor all your days in crying repentance unto this people, and bring, save it be one soul unto me, how great shall be your joy with him in the kingdom of my Father!" (D&C 18:15.)

God's greatest gift is eternal life. In 1837, when darkness, wickedness, and confusion came to many, the Prophet Joseph Smith's mind was clear. He was not confused. He could expertly determine right from wrong. His inspiration from the Lord was certain.

Heber C. Kimball's mind also was clear. He knew what was right and what was wrong. He was resolute in pursuing right no matter what the personal cost or loss. Those whom Satan influenced were loudly proclaiming falsehoods, confusing many basically good people who thought they were doing right, even doing God's will, but they were not.

That which protects the mind is the helmet of salvation. Joseph Smith, Heber C. Kimball, and Brigham Young, among others, had it on. With it, they were protected against all the false ideas and concepts of the day, and they could make decisions clearly. To us also today, the way is clear if we are wearing the helmet of salvation. We need only ask, Is it right? If it is right, we will pursue the course no matter what is required.

While a Roman helmet was attractive, it was also very practical. Decorated on top with horse hair, it curved down over the neck so that the neck as well as the head was protected. Hanging from both sides were pieces of leather that protected the cheeks. The helmet was tough enough to withstand the blows of the enemy's two-edge swords and the archer's arrows. One would be foolish to go into battle without his helmet securely in place, and one would make every effort and take every precaution to make certain it stayed in place during the battle.

The spiritual helmet that is worn by the soldier of the Great King Jesus Christ is salvation. President Harold B. Lee taught as follows:

> And now finally to the last piece of the prophet-teacher's armored dress. We will put a helmet upon the head. Our head or our intellect is the controlling member of our body. It must be well protected against the enemy. . . . But now in order for this helmet to be effective, it must be of an exquisite design. It must be of a super-material to be effective in our eternal conflict with the invisible enemy of all righteousness. Ours is to be the "helmet of salvation." Salvation means the attainment of the eternal right to live in the presence of God the Father and the Son as a reward for a good life in mortality.
>
> With the goal of salvation ever in our mind's eye as the ultimate to be achieved, our thinking and our decisions which determine action will always challenge all that would jeopardize that glorious future state. Lost indeed is that soul who is intellectually without the "helmet of salvation." (*Stand Ye in Holy Places,* pp. 334-35.)

To put the helmet of salvation on one's head is to resist the sophistry, the false logic, the false reasoning, the pride, the egotism of men. To do this, the plan of salvation must be internalized within us.

The plan of salvation is not complex. It is available to all, and all have or can have the capacity to understand it. We need to learn and remember it well. Our difficulties come if we forget it, for our enemy attempts continually to raise questions and doubts and blot from our minds the purpose and mission that determine our immediate and our future conduct.

The Prophet Joseph Smith received the following from the Lord on March 8, 1831:

But ye are commanded in all things to ask of God, who giveth liberally; and that which the Spirit testifies unto you even so I would that ye should do in all holiness of heart, walking uprightly before me, considering the end of your salvation, doing all things with prayer and thanksgiving, that ye may not be seduced by evil spirits, or doctrines of devils, or the commandments of men; for some are of men, and others of devils. (D&C 46:7.)

Among other things, if we walk uprightly before God and consider the end of our salvation, we will not be seduced by doctrines of devils or commandments of men. We cannot fully consider and appreciate the end of our salvation without knowing also about the beginning of our salvation.

Man is an eternal being. His existence did not begin with birth nor does it end with death. All of us are literally children of God, our Father in heaven. We dwelled with him in a premortal state. We were taught by him; we learned, we progressed, and we experienced great joy with him.

In our pre-earth life we were anxious to be more like our Father. He had a glorious body of flesh and bones. We loved and admired him and wanted to be like him. A plan was devised whereby an earth was created for us and we were to go to it, obtain bodies, and have opportunity for growth and development. We were to have opposition so that growth and development would be possible; that is, there was to be evil as well as good on the earth. If we lived up to our potential as children of God, we could return to his presence; if we did not live up to our potential, we could not return to him.

Our Father in heaven and his Son Jesus Christ loved us too much not to do all in their power to assist us. It was determined that Jesus, our Elder Brother and the great God who had created this earth under the direction of the Father, would come down to this earth and would be born in the lowliest of temporal circumstances. Thus he was born of Mary in a manger in a stable. His mother, Mary, was mortal; his father was God, our Father in heaven. Jesus was subject to temptations and suffering and pain. (See Mosiah 3; Alma 7.) But despite all that happened to him, he remained totally sinless. He overcame the evil and all the problems of the world. No one else who had ever lived had done that, and no one else who would ever live could.

Jesus, who overcame the world, extends his love, mercy, and power to us if we will obey him. Alone, we cannot overcome the world; with our Savior's help, we can.

As much as our Father in heaven and the Savior both love us, they will never force us to follow them. We may choose throughout our entire lives to do as they would like us to and we will receive the blessings that follow; or we may reject and live our lives apart from their help and guidance and the help and guidance of their servants on the earth. This is "free agency"; all may choose the course they will take.

As each of us leaves this earthly existence by a process called death, the spirit, which lived before, is separated from the physical body. We continue to be the same individuals, but we are separated temporarily from the physical body. Those who have been obedient in mortality go to paradise, a place of joy and opportunities for continued service to God and fellow beings. Those who have been disobedient to the Savior's teachings while on this earth go to a place of departed spirits called spirit prison.

The soul of a person is comprised of the body and the spirit. The reuniting of the body and spirit takes place at the resurrection of the body from the grave. Jesus was the first to be resurrected, and by him and through him all persons are resurrected and live forever. All will stand to be judged of him. Those who were valiant in his cause and who lived his gospel will dwell with him and with our Father eternally. Others will enter the celestial kingdom but will not be exalted with the blessing of eternal lives.

Some will be assigned to the terrestrial kingdom;

"these are they who are not valiant in the testimony of Jesus." (D&C 76:79.) Some will be assigned to a lesser kingdom, the telestial. "These are they who are liars, and sorcerers, and adulterers, and whoremongers, and whosoever loves and makes a lie." (D&C 76:103.)

The gospel is designed to bring God's children to exaltation in the celestial kingdom to dwell with him eternally as his sons and daughters. God has given no plan to follow to receive a lesser inheritance because he wants none to have a lesser inheritance. Those who obtain less do so because of disobedience.

The gospel plan is simple. The Savior said: "Behold I have given unto you my gospel, and this is the gospel which I have given unto you—that I came into the world to do the will of my Father, because my Father sent me." (3 Nephi 27:13.) This verse is followed by the story of the plan of salvation, outlined in simple terms. Satan, our enemy, would have us forget this plan and not live by it, because the only way we may obtain our salvation, the only way we may be saved and exalted in the celestial kingdom, is by living according to it.

To have eternal life, we must seek it. There are those who do not find it because their focus is to the future only, and eternal things are to be gained in the present. Eternal things cannot be obtained by the sweep of God's hand; they are fashioned hour by hour, day by day. Simple things, uncomplex things, may become eternal things.

In this life we need those things which sustain the body and bring physical comfort. But to have a fulness of life, we must seek eternal things—those which continue with the individual and can pass through the gate of death with us. Eternity is here and now, on a day-by-day basis. It requires seeking, improving, and magnifying—not only ourselves, but also helping others to do the same.

Cannot man's mind reach out and grasp the obvious, or is it too close at hand, too simple to be understood? Cannot we take our Savior as a model of one who sought and obtained those things which are of eternal value? We recall his gentleness to a child, his tenderness to a sinner, his forgiveness of one who was being ridiculed. Stopping to comfort an injured person was not an infringement on the time of his mission—it *was* his mission. It was not an intrusion on time that was to be spent on important work—it *was* the important work.

How do we best visualize our Lord on the earth? Healing the ear of one who came to take him. (Luke 22:50-51.) Asking a follower to care for his mother, Mary. (John 19:26-27.) Entreating his Father in heaven to forgive his assailants. (Luke 23:34.) Then, three days later, we see him living in what we refer to as eternity. A resurrected being, he returns again to be with his disciples. Let us now consider his behavior.

He tells his disciples where to cast their nets to obtain food. (John 21:6.) He instructs Peter to care for his followers. (John 21:15-17.) He blesses Thomas, who believes because he has seen, and he instructs his followers as to the merits of believing without seeing. (John 20:26-29.)

Eternity is now; the present is reality. For some the future may be an illusion; it may be the protector of the indolent and the hope of the procrastinator. To such the future will prove futile because it always remains the future, to be grasped after but just beyond reach.

Great deeds and great acts must always be fashioned out of the inconvenience of today, the impossibleness of the present moment. There may never be an opportune time, an ideal moment. The time to do great tasks, think great thoughts, and achieve is the only time there is—now.

Man has limitations; God has none. As man extends himself, God enlarges him. The hours of the day remain the same, but man's ability to do continues to increase through the power of God. Herein lies the secret of the man who grasps the eternal. He does it now with the help of an all-powerful God. Another person may wait and wait until the future when there is time, but that time never comes. When that which was future and looked so opportune, so desirable, so effortless finally arrives and is converted into the now, it also is filled with reality, with problems, with frustrations. But if one looks carefully, with a discerning eye, it is filled also with promise and with opportunity.

Let us thank God for eternal things, that we can recognize and grasp them in the here and now, and that they may forever be a part of us—things selected at inconvenient, sometimes painful moments when other less important things would have crowded them out forever if we had permitted them to do so.

Like the Savior, we may accumulate and take much of the eternal with us, and thus it is no mystery how we may have eternal life. The Savior points the way. "I am the way, the truth, and the life," he said. (John 14:6.) "And whosoever liveth and believeth in me shall never die." (John 11:26.) If we live and believe in him, we shall live in eternal abundance, much of it gleaned along the path of life, a life some find inconvenient but others fashion into opportunity from the minutes and the hours of a seemingly unspectacular day. The resistance an individual encounters when he seeks to convert the now into the eternal can be almost devastating. Hence, we see the need of power beyond our own, the power of God. We must put on the helmet of salvation now. To live with the intention of putting it on someday is most dangerous.

President Joseph F. Smith spoke of two classes of people in the Church:

Among the Latter-day Saints, the preaching of false doctrines disguised as truths of the gospel, may be expected from people of two classes, and practically from these only; they are:

First—the hopelessly ignorant, whose lack of intelligence is due to their indolence and sloth, who make but feeble effort, if indeed any at all, to better themselves by reading and study; those who are afflicted with a dread disease that may develop into an incurable malady—laziness.

Second—the proud and self vaunting ones, who read by. the lamp of their own conceit; who interpret by rules of their own contriving; who have become a law unto themselves, and so pose as the sole judges of their own doings. More dangerously ignorant than the first.

Beware of the lazy and the proud. . . . (*Gospel Doctrine,* p. 373.)

Satan is able to seduce these two different groups, some by not using their minds and others by using their minds and being proud of it, feeling superior, and being disobedient to the Lord and his servants. These two groups, though vastly different, both lack one most important part of the armor—the helmet of salvation—to protect their intellect.

Oliver Cowdery was an intelligent man, but he permitted himself to be deceived. Wilford Woodruff, speaking of Oliver's apostasy, said:

I passed through that scene [great apostasy in Kirtland], as did some others who are now with us. . . . Even Apostles took occasion to rise up and endeavored to dictate and direct the Prophet of God. . . . Those who testified to the Book of Mormon were led away through not keeping the commandments of God and thinking that they themselves were great men. Some of them were learned men; some of them considered themselves very smart men, and they were so smart that they wanted to dictate and direct the Prophet of God. The consequence of all this was that they turned aside from the commandments of God. Some of them had been true and faithful in their labors in the ministry. I have heard Oliver Cowdery testify of the Book of Mormon by the power of God, when it seemed as if the very earth trembled under his feet. He was filled with the Holy Ghost and the power of God while he was faithful, and so were many of these men. But Oliver Cowdery yielded to the temptation of the evil one, and we may say he apostatized. So did Martin Harris, and several others connected with them. They left the Church, they turned against Joseph, and they said he was a fallen prophet, and they themselves wanted to direct the Church. . . . Several of these men called upon me in the time of this apostasy and asked me to join them against the Prophet; the Prophet was fallen, they said. Now, I had seen enough myself of the Prophet of God, and I had read enough of the revelations of

God through him, to know that he was a Prophet of God, and not a fallen prophet. I saw that these men were yielding to the devil, and I told them so. Said I: "You will all go to hell unless you repent. Joseph has been raised up by the power of God, . . . he has been true and faithful to God and to the Church and kingdom of God here on the earth. . . ." (*Millennial Star*, May 30, 1895, 57:339-40.)

Wilford Woodruff was protected by the helmet of salvation. Oliver Cowdery and Martin Harris could have been but they were not. Some persons today, like Oliver Cowdery, think that they are in advance of the prophet of the Lord. They are not. They have just misplaced their helmets. Others are too lazy to learn, to assist, and to care, and this too is a result of misplaced helmets.

The helmet of salvation helps us maintain proper knowledge, gratitude, and perspective. How can we become lifted up in the pride of our own little intellectual or temporal accomplishments when we reflect upon the meekness of the greatest of all, the Savior, and consider our own nothingness and our dependence upon him? Nephi said:

For we labor diligently to write, to persuade our children, and also our brethren, to believe in Christ, and to be reconciled to God; for we know that it is by grace that we are saved, after all we can do. . . .

And we talk of Christ, we rejoice in Christ, we preach of Christ, we prophesy of Christ, and we write according to our prophecies, that our children may know to what source they may look for a remission of their sins. (2 Nephi 25:23, 26.)

The Lord declared: "The glory of God is intelligence" (D&C 93:36), and "it is impossible for a man to be saved in ignorance" (D&C 131:6). We should all learn to the fullest extent of our ability, but the helmet of salvation must be securely in place at all times so that we will be assets to the kingdom of God and not liabilities. A church member cannot be intelligent without the protection of the Lord's helmet. Nearly every Latter-day Saint will at some point in life come up against a problem that cannot be handled intellectually.

If the helmet of salvation is in place it will not be difficult to rely on the first principle of the gospel for help and strength. The glory of God is intelligence, and this is a great truth, but faith in the Lord Jesus Christ is the first principle of the gospel. If we do not rely on faith, alienation or apostasy may follow.

If in our thoughts we find ourselves—not the Lord and the building of his kingdom—on center stage, we should be concerned. We should examine our helmet for holes. The archenemy who is concerned about no one save himself may have gained entrance to our minds and be in the process of using an approach that will lead us from peace of mind and happiness and ultimate righteousness into dissatisfaction and sorrow. This old approach begins with admiration for oneself. The individual sees himself as perceptive, thoughtful, and clever when compared to most others. But as time passes, he becomes blinded by his own supposed luster, loses his way, and starts on a downward path. He may find little on that downward path to elevate his thoughts and actions, and with the passing of years self-admiration may well turn to self-contempt. Sadly, in the intervening time many loved ones and friends may have been alienated, their hearts broken. This may add to the ever-widening, pitiful circle that eventually may engulf the deceived one.

There is a price to pay in securing in place the helmet of salvation. This price includes time, energy, concentration, effort, prayer, self-evaluation, reevaluation, and repentance; but as high as the price is, it is small compared with the cost of not putting the helmet on.

Knowledge, especially gospel knowledge, opens avenues of service, enjoyment, and satisfaction that those who knowingly choose to remain ignorant may never know; it is also impossible for one to govern himself if he has never learned correct principles.

Joseph Smith was a superb example of one who

hungered and thirsted after knowledge. This example set by the first prophet of this dispensation continues with our present beloved prophet. That hunger to learn should be in each of us.

Good books and magazines should be among our most cherished possessions. We should be extremely reluctant to conclude that we do not have the time, money, energy, or ability to continue the educational process either formally or informally. There is much to be said for self-education. Some persons I admire most have fashioned excellent self-education programs when formal educational opportunities were denied them. It is not a sacrifice to gain an education; the real sacrifice is in not gaining one. And as we continue to learn and to use righteously the knowledge we gain, there is a continuing air of excitement present in life, for we will find ourselves on the path to our ultimate goal—immortality and eternal life.

Chapter 8

THE SWORD
OF THE SPIRIT

And the sword of the Spirit,
which is the word of God. (Ephesians 6:17.)
. . . and the sword of my Spirit,
which I will pour out upon you, and my word
which I reveal unto you. . . . (D&C 27:18.)

The Roman sword was about thirty-three inches long, two-edged, sharp-pointed, and used for thrusting. Like any sword, it could be used in many different ways. It could be used to provide food for the hungry and to protect the innocent and the defenseless from greed, lust, and viciousness. It may be used to defend the cause of truth, right, and justice. It was a useful instrument in the hands of a just, noble man.

The sword is used by the Lord as a symbol for the word of God. His word as it came from his own mouth was used in a variety of ways, depending upon his purposes. He spoke gently and reassuringly to Mary and Martha about their brother Lazarus. (John 11:1-46.) To the servant of Jairus he used warm and tender words. (Luke 8:41-48.) He spoke sharply to Peter: "Get thee behind me, Satan." (Matthew 16:23.) He rebuked the smug and self-righteous Pharisees: "Wo unto you, scribes and Pharisees, hypocrites!" (Matthew 23:15.)

The Savior's love for all is unquestioned. His mission is to save all mankind, and so the way he spoke to people was determined by their eternal needs. While he was on the earth he chose and trained disciples who were to carry on his great saving work. Prior to his departure, he promised them that they would receive the Holy Ghost to comfort them and to guide them in carrying out the work of God's kingdom on the earth. "But the Comforter, which is the Holy Ghost, whom the Father will send in my name, he shall teach you all things, and bring all things to your remembrance, whatsoever I have said unto you." (John 14:26.) He further taught: "But when the Comforter is come, whom I will send unto you from the Father, even the Spirit of truth, which proceedeth from the Father, he shall testify of me." (John 15:26.)

The Savior promised his disciples: "Howbeit when he, the Spirit of truth, is come, he will guide you into all truth: for he shall not speak of himself; but whatsoever he shall hear, that shall he speak: and he will shew you things to come. He shall glorify me: for he shall receive of mine, and shall shew it unto you." (John 16:13-14.)

If we are desirous and worthy, the Holy Ghost, the Spirit of truth, will bring all things to our remembrance, testify of the Savior, show us things to come, and take of the things of the Savior and reveal them unto us.

We are to utilize the Holy Ghost, the Spirit of the Lord, when we teach. In modern-day revelation we learn: "And the Spirit shall be given unto you by the prayer of faith; and if ye receive not the Spirit ye shall not teach." (D&C 42:14.)

In reality, if we do not have the Spirit we cannot teach the things of God, but are left to ourselves to teach the things of man. This is stated very clearly by the Lord in section 50 of the Doctrine and Covenants: "Verily I say unto you, he that is ordained of me and sent forth to preach the word of truth by the Comforter, in the Spirit of truth, doth he preach it by the Spirit of truth or some other way? And if it be by some other way it is not of God." (D&C 50:17-18.)

The Lord in his holy scriptures has admonished us to obtain his word. In D&C 130:19 he tells us that it is obtained by "diligence and obedience." In D&C 11:21 we are counseled to seek first to obtain the Lord's word and then to declare it. The Lord refers to his word as "the sword of my Spirit." That sword, the word of God, must be learned and used as he dictates through his Spirit.

The Lord has instructed us: ". . . treasure up in your minds continually the words of life, and it shall be given you in the very hour that portion that shall be meted unto every man." (D&C 84:85.) One meaning of treasure is "to put away securely for future use." A treasure is, of course, something that is precious.

The Lord may quicken our mental ability so that we can reach into our mental storehouse and recall exactly the information that is most pertinent for a particular situation. With the companionship of the Holy Ghost and under his directing influence, that which we say becomes the word of God through us at that specific time. Brigham Young spoke of a most important experience in his life:

> If all the talent, tact, wisdom, and refinement of the world had been sent to me with the Book of Mormon, and had declared, in the most exalted of earthly eloquence, the truth of it, undertaking to prove it by learning and worldly wisdom, they would have been to me like the smoke which arises only to vanish away. But when I saw a man without eloquence, or talents for public speaking, who could only say, "I know, by the power of the Holy Ghost, that the Book of Mormon is true, that Joseph Smith is a Prophet of the Lord," the Holy Ghost proceeding from that individual illuminated my understanding, and light, glory, and immortality were before me. I was encircled by them, filled with them, and I knew for myself that the testimony of the man was true. But the wisdom of the world, I say again, is like smoke, like the fog of the night, that disappears before the rays of the luminary of the day, or like the hoar-frost in the warmth of the sun's rays. My own judgment, natural endowments, and education bowed to this simple, but

mighty testimony. There sits the man who baptized me, (brother Eleazer Miller.) It filled my system with light, and my soul with joy. The world, with all its wisdom and power, and with all the glory and gilded show of its kings or potentates, sinks into perfect insignificance, compared with the simple, unadorned testimony of the servant of God. (*Journal of Discourses* 1:90-91.)

Eleazer Miller had treasured up that which Brigham Young needed to know, and the word of God came from his mouth as powerful as a two-edged sword, cutting asunder false tradition and ideas and pricking Brigham Young's heart and touching his soul.

The sword of the Spirit, the word of God, must be sought diligently, by study, by prayer, and by listening to church leaders, and then used as the Lord directs to save his children.

President John Taylor was sensitive to the promptings of the Spirit of the Lord, the word of God inside him, and under the Lord's direction he solved a very serious problem in a simple and beautiful way. Heber J. Grant tells this wonderful story from President Taylor's life:

I recall one incident showing how song has the power to soothe irritated feelings and bring harmony to the hearts of men who are filled with a contentious spirit. It occurred many years ago, and involved a quarrel between two old and faithful brethren whose membership dated back to the days of Nauvoo. These men had been full of integrity and devotion to the work of the Lord. They had been through many of the hardships of Nauvoo, and had suffered the drivings and persecutions of the Saints, as well as the hardships of pioneering incident to the early settlement of the West. These men had quarreled over some business affairs, and finally concluded that they would try to get President John Taylor to help them adjust their difficulties.

John Taylor was then the president of the Council of the Twelve Apostles. These brethren pledged their word of honor that they would faithfully abide by whatever decision Brother Taylor might render. . . .

Accordingly they called on President Taylor, but did not immediately tell him what their trouble was, but explained that they had seriously quarreled and asked him if he would listen to their story and render his decision. President Taylor willingly consented.

But he said: "Brethren, before I hear your case, I would like very much to sing one of the songs of Zion for you."

Now President Taylor was a very capable singer, and interpreted sweetly and with spirit, our sacred hymns. He sang one of our hymns to the two brethren. Seeing its effect, he remarked that he never heard one of the songs of Zion but that he wanted to listen to one more, and so asked them to listen while he sang another. Of course, they consented. They both seemed to enjoy it; and, having sung the second song, he remarked that he had heard there is luck in odd numbers and so with their consent he would sing still another, which he did. Then, in his jocular way, he remarked: "Now, brethren, I do not want to wear you out, but if you will forgive me, and listen to one more hymn, I promise to stop singing, and will hear your case."

The story goes that when President Taylor had finished the fourth song, the brethren were melted to tears, got up, shook hands, and asked President Taylor to excuse them for having called upon him, and for taking up his time. They then departed without his even knowing what their difficulties were.

President Taylor's singing had reconciled their feelings toward each other. The Spirit of the Lord had entered their hearts, and the hills of difference that rose between them had been leveled and become as nothing. Love and brotherhood had developed in their souls, and the trifles over which they had quarreled, had become of no consequence in their sight. The songs of the heart had filled them with the spirit of reconciliation. (*Improvement Era*, September 1940, p. 522.)

The Lord knew exactly how to handle the situation. The word of God through John Taylor was as a sword cutting away suspicion, distrust, and bitterness, permitting the two men to once again become brothers in the gospel of Jesus Christ. The word of God, the sword of the Spirit, must be used exactly right in each situation so that the maximum good can result. If we are well prepared, humble, and inspired of the Lord, this can be so as we do the Lord's work.

Elder Alonzo A. Hinckley was willing to serve the Lord with all the intensity of his soul. Once he was separated from his wife and child and diligently doing the Lord's work in Holland. He wrote of this experience:

... I had never sought for a sign ... but I did seek the Spirit of the Lord to help me touch the hearts of men. I not only prayed to the Lord to assist me to learn the Dutch language, but I also studied it as faithfully as I could. I succeeded in learning two or three sentences which enabled me to deliver my literature from door to door.

One day, when I was alone, visiting among the people at Rotterdam, it was my duty to go back to the homes in which I had left tracts and take up the literature. As I went to gather the booklets, some power, that I cannot understand, possessed me until I quaked and trembled. I stood and looked at the house at which I was to call and felt as if I could not go to the door. But I knew my duty and so, with fortitude and determination I went to the house, raised the knocker and dropped it. Almost instantly, the door opened and an irate woman stepped out and closed it behind her. She talked in a very loud, shrill voice, berating me most severely.

I did not realize for the moment, that I was understanding Dutch as clearly as though she had been speaking English. I felt no supernatural power, or influence, or feeling. I just knew every word she was saying. She spoke so loudly that a carpenter, who was working across the street, building a porch on a little store, heard her and, I suppose, thought I was abusing the woman, for he came over to where we stood and brought his son with him and, greatly to my alarm, he carried a broadax. The man took his position near me and listened to the woman, who continued her tirade against me in a shouting voice.

I did not grow angry because of the woman's abuse, but to the contrary, my soul was filled with a burning desire to speak her language and to testify of the divinity of the Gospel and of the Lord Jesus Christ. I thought if I could only explain to her the importance of my message and the good it would do her, she would not berate me as she does now.

In a few moments she ceased her abuse and I began speaking. And I spoke the Dutch language. I defended the Truth and bore testimony of the restoration of the Gospel.

I had forgotten the large man who stood near me with his ax, and, as I looked at the woman and delivered my message of truth, he put his arms across my shoulders, and, looking the woman in the face, said, "The Mormon Church may have its black sheep, but this is a man of God."

Her bitterness now gone, the woman replied, "I know it." (Bryant S. Hinckley, *The Faith of Our Pioneer Fathers* [Deseret Book, 1959], pp. 231-33.)

The word of God, the sword of the Spirit, was used by Elder Hinckley to teach the truth, to dispel bitterness, and to establish peace in the heart of a Dutch woman who had been deceived.

This is a day when God's servants need to be bold, which is synonymous with being daring, courageous, and fearless. In writing to the Ephesians, Paul asked the saints for their prayers, "that I may open my mouth boldly. . . . For I am an ambassador," he said, "that therein I may speak boldly, as I ought to speak." (Ephesians 6:20.)

Paul tells us to put on the whole armor of God and then to be bold and to speak boldly. The Lord in our day has said: "Contend thou, therefore, morning by morning; and day after day let thy warning voice go forth; and when the night cometh let not the inhabitants of the earth slumber, because of thy speech." (D&C 112:5.)

The Lord is displeased with those who will not boldly preach his gospel. He has said: "But with some I am not well pleased, for they will not open their mouths, but they hide the talent which I have given unto them, because of the fear of man. Wo unto such, for mine anger is kindled against them." (D&C 60:2.)

If the Prophet Joseph Smith had failed to be bold, his voice would have been drowned out by the loud voices of his enemies. However, he was never intimidated by the shouting voices of falsehood. He boldly proclaimed the glad tidings of the restored gospel throughout his life. In the Carthage Jail he boldly proclaimed the truth to those who guarded him.

President Jedediah M. Grant exemplifies the attitude and commitment of a bold soldier in God's army:

I tell you that the devil is working against us, and Lucifer is in the land . . . the same Lucifer that was cast down from heaven. . . . But thanks be to our God, and to high heaven, the light of God is here and the truth of God is here, and we have waged a war with Lucifer, under the banner of the Lord Jesus Christ. May we be able to stand in the contest and overcome. . . . We say to you, Saints, rub up your armor, gird on the sword of the Almighty and walk forth to battle, and never yield the ground.

85

Some men say that they feel sick and faint, and weary, when they see so much darkness among the people. I feel as though I could say to the mountains and to all hell, get out of my way, or I will kick you out; I am not going to surrender. . . .

I am not of that class that believes in shrinking; if there is a fight on hand, give me a share of it. I am naturally good natured, but when the indignation of the Almighty is in me I say to all hell, stand aside and let the Lord Jesus Christ come in here; He shall be heir of the earth; the truth shall triumph, the Priesthood and Christ shall reign. . . .

And by the power of the Priesthood restored by the Prophet Joseph, by the light of heaven shed forth by brother Brigham and his associates, we expect to triumph; and in the name of Jesus Christ, we do not mean to surrender to evil. (*Journal of Discourses* 4:86-87.)

We live in a day when an overbearing and brazen enemy is arrayed against us. The Lord needs all of us with our swords to boldly strike out against evil and defend that which is true and right. The enemy must be met with fearlessness and courage, for nothing else will bring success.

President Wilford Woodruff is famous for effectively using the sword of the Spirit, the word of God. He had been sent to England to preach the word of God, and preach the word of God he would. He wrote:

On Sunday, the 8th, I preached at Frome's Hill in the morning, at Standley Hill in the afternoon, and at John Benbow's, Hill Farm, in the evening.

The parish church that stood in the neighborhood of Brother Benbow's, presided over by the rector of the parish, was attended during the day by only fifteen persons, while I had a large congregation, estimated to number a thousand, attend my meetings through the day and evening.

When I arose to speak at Brother Benbow's house, a man entered the door and informed me that he was a constable, and had been sent by the rector of the parish with a warrant to arrest me. I asked him, "For what crime?" He said, "For preaching to the people." I told him that I, as well as the rector, had a license for preaching the gospel to the people, and that if he would take a chair I would wait upon him after the meeting. He took my chair and sat beside me. For an hour and a quarter I preached the first principles of the everlasting gospel. The power of God rested upon me, the Spirit filled the house, and the people were convinced. At the close of the meeting I opened the door for baptism, and seven offered themselves. Among the number were four preachers and the constable. The latter arose and said, "Mr. Woodruff, I would like to be baptized." I told him I would like to baptize him. I went down to the pool and baptized the seven. We then came together. I confirmed thirteen, administered the Sacrament, and we all rejoiced together.

The constable went to the rector and told him that if he wanted Mr. Woodruff taken for preaching the gospel, he must go himself and serve the writ; for he had heard him preach the only true gospel sermon he had ever listened to in his life. The rector did not know what to make of it, so he sent two clerks of the Church of England as spies, to attend our meeting, and find out what we did preach. They were both pricked in their hearts, and received the word of the Lord gladly, and were baptized and confirmed members of the Church of Jesus Christ of Latter-day Saints. The rector became alarmed and did not dare to send anybody else. (Matthias F. Cowley, *Wilford Woodruff, History of His Life and Labors* [Deseret News, 1909], pp. 117-18.)

Elder Woodruff had the Spirit of God in him, and therefore he was bold in saving souls. A servant of God cannot be bold if he does not have that same Spirit.

A soldier who went into battle without a sword would be reluctant, evasive, and frightened. He would be looking for a fellow soldier armed with a sword to protect him.

One who does not have the word of God may well develop a similar desire to let someone else do it. To be bold we must have the word of God inside us in our hearts and minds so that we may teach positively and forcefully.

Two elders who were transferred to an Indian reservation rode through the reservation with the departing elders and asked about the families in each house. After a time a specific house was singled out. "Who lives there?" "We don't know," came the reply. "We do know, however, that the last elders who were here were met at the door of that house with a rifle and warned that if missionaries ever returned they would be shot."

A few days later the two missionaries after prayerful

consideration approached the door of that house. When the door was opened, they boldly declared who they were and why they were there. To their surprise they were not greeted by someone who was hostile, but by a family that had lived in that house for only a few weeks. They were receptive to the gospel and were baptized within a short time. A few months later when a little chapel was built and a branch of the Church organized, the husband and father who lived in the long-feared house became the branch president.

We cannot let Satan intimidate us. We must keep our sword sharp by study, meditation, prayer, repentance, and Church service.

One of my favorite stories from Church history took place in 1856. Joseph F. Smith, just nineteen years old, was returning from a mission to Hawaii. En route home, in California, he and others stopped for the night and made camp.

It was at the time of the Utah war, and feelings were running high. Joseph Fielding Smith relates his father's experience:

One day after the little company of wagons had traveled a short distance and made their camp, a company of drunken men rode into the camp on horseback, cursing and swearing and threatening to kill any "Mormons" that came within their path. It was the lot of Joseph F. Smith to meet these marauders first. Some of the brethren when they heard them coming had cautiously gone into the brush down the creek, out of sight, where they waited for this band to pass. Joseph F. was a little distance from the camp gathering wood for the fire when these men rode up. When he saw them, he said, his first thought was to do what the other brethren had done, and seek shelter in the trees and in flight. Then the thought came to him, "Why should I run from these fellows?" With that thought in mind he boldly marched up with his arms full of wood to the campfire. As he was about to deposit his wood, one of the ruffians, still with his pistols in his hands and pointing at the youthful Elder, and cursing as only a drunken rascal can, declaring that it was his duty to exterminate every "Mormon" he should meet, demanded in a loud, angry voice, "Are you a 'Mormon'?"

Without a moment of hesitation and looking the ruffian in the eye, Joseph F. Smith boldly answered, "Yes, siree; dyed in the wool; true blue, through and through."

The answer was given boldly and without any sign of fear, which completely disarmed the belligerent man, and in his bewilderment, he grasped the missionary by the hand and said: "Well, you are the _____ _____ pleasantest man I ever met! Shake, young fellow, I am glad to see a man that stands up for his convictions." . . .

This man, evidently the leader of the band, then rode off, the others following him. . . . (Joseph Fielding Smith, *Life of Joseph F. Smith* [Deseret Book Co., 1938], pp. 188-89.)

One cannot use the sword if he does not have it. We must obtain the sword, the word of God, and use it effectively as did John Taylor, Alonzo A. Hinckley, Wilford Woodruff, and Joseph F. Smith. The sword of the Spirit is a most noble weapon in the hands of a righteous, well-informed person.

The word of God must always be used humbly and for the purpose for which it is intended. It should be used to bind up the wounds of the grieving, help deliver the captive from his sins, help protect the innocent from temptation, prick the conscience of the slothful, and as a protection in the work of the Lord. As we learn more, gain more experience, and become more faithful, the Lord will entrust us to use more and more the word of his mouth, the sword of his Spirit.

We are soldiers in God's army; we wear his armor. We have his sword, his word. We have been given our objective: to defeat Satan, our enemy, and all his forces and establish the Lord's righteousness on the earth. This cannot be done unless we are adept at using the sword and using it boldly all the days of our lives.

Each of us must have the sword, the word of God, in his life to successfully cut through the snares of the devil and save himself and assist in saving others. Each of us must follow the counsel of Helaman:

"Yea, we see that whosoever will may lay hold upon the word of God, which is quick and powerful, which shall divide asunder all the cunning and the snares and the wiles of the devil, and lead the man of Christ in a straight and narrow course across that everlasting gulf of misery which is prepared to engulf the wicked—

"And land their souls, yea, their immortal souls, at the right hand of God in the kingdom of heaven, to sit down with Abraham, and Isaac, and with Jacob, and with all our holy fathers, to go no more out." (Helaman 3:29-30.)

Chapter 9

PRAYING ALWAYS

*Praying always with all prayer
and supplication in the Spirit. . . .
(Ephesians 6:18.)
". . . and be agreed as touching all things
whatsoever ye ask of me. . . .
(D&C 27:18.)*

Daniel, a Jew, in exile had arisen to an enviable position in the eyes of his associates. He was next in authority to King Darius, and the king's many other counselors plotted against him to remove him from his position. Daniel was preferred by the king because "an excellent spirit was in him."

Those who plotted against Daniel could find no error or fault in him and finally determined that the only way they could find "occasion" against him was concerning the law of his God. They knew he would obey his God before he would obey any man. They proceeded to flatter the king, who ignorantly signed a proclamation decreeing that for a period of thirty days no petition could go to anyone except the king, thus giving him proper honor for his greatness. The penalty for disobedience was certain death in the lions' den.

At the appointed hour for prayer Daniel sent up his petition to God as he always had, knowing full well what the consequences would be. His enemies heard and took him to the king, who, though much grieved, had Daniel cast into the lions' den and sealed the door. The king spent a sleepless night and at daybreak ran to the den and called out, "O Daniel, servant of the living God, is thy God, whom thou servest continually, able to deliver thee from the lions?" Daniel, unharmed, replied to the king's query with this significant statement: "My God hath sent his angel, and hath shut the lions' mouths, that they have not hurt me: forasmuch as before him innocency was found in me; and also before thee, O king, have I done no hurt." (See Daniel 6.)

Daniel's attitude is a fascinating one. It has always impressed me that he would rather face hungry lions than try to live for thirty days without communication with God.

Another story that I have long known and appreciated was told by an apostle of God, Marriner W. Merrill.

In the winter of 1855, Elder Merrill was cutting red pine logs in a canyon close to Salt Lake City. One very icy morning he hitched his oxen to his sled and drove to the site of the pine trees. There he worked rapidly in order to keep warm and so he could get home early. After cutting five pine logs and sliding them down the hill, with great difficulty he was able to load one on the sled. But as he turned to get another log, the first log slipped from the sled and pinned him across the other logs. The pain was excruciating, and he began to lose consciousness. He knew that if he did, he would freeze to death.

Elder Merrill prayed fervently that the Lord would see him in his plight and spare his life. Then he lapsed into unconsciousness. When he came to, he was seated on top of his load of logs and his oxen were moving down the canyon. He was sitting upon his sheepskin coat, and since it was so cold, he decided to jump down and put it on. But when he attempted to get off the logs, he found he could not move his legs, so he put his coat around him as best he could and continued toward home.

Because Elder Merrill was late in arriving home his wife, anxious for his safety, was waiting in the yard. With difficulty, she helped him into the house. It was several days before he could walk. After telling this faith-promoting story, Elder Merrill concluded:

I have hesitated to narrate this incident because of the skepticism which is so common at the present day, even among some who profess to be Saints, concerning things somewhat supernatural; but I can truthfully testify in all soberness, that some power which I did not see assisted me from the position which doubtless would have speedily cost me my life. As I was preserved for some purpose known to my Heavenly Father, so do I also believe that God will bless and preserve the lives of his faithful children, just as long as it is necessary for them to live to accomplish their missions upon the earth. (Preston Nibley, comp., *Pioneer Stories* [Deseret News Press, 1952], pp. 55-56.)

Elder Merrill, like Daniel, found himself in a position where he needed God, where he himself could not do anything about the situation.

We cannot live very long and not need God's intervention in our lives. Our need may not be as dramatic as was Daniel's or Marriner W. Merrill's—to them it was literally a matter of life or death—but to us it may make the difference between happiness and unhappiness, success and failure, spiritual progress and spiritual retrogression.

Our Father in heaven loves us. He sent us to this beautiful earth. Many, however, have not kept his commandments, resulting in unhappiness. Some have gone so far as to deny the existence of our Heavenly Father; they do not know him or feel his presence in their lives, and then they wrongly generalize that if they and others like themselves do not know him, no one does, and therefore he does not exist. The obedient children know that he lives; they also know of his great love and his eagerness to assist and bless us.

Our Father in heaven is perfect. He has all knowledge, infinite love, and infinite power. I am grateful to know that my Father in heaven is perfect. His love for all of us is perfect, and his power is without limitation. We know, then, that he not only loves us, but he also has the power to bring to pass his desires for us if, of course, we are worthy and do our part. This knowledge can give each of us a wonderful sense of peace, security, and unlimited confidence in carrying out his desires. We lived in his presence, but to be tried, tested, and gain earthly experience and to continue our eternal progression, we came to this earth.

Part of the plan was that we would lose our memories of the premortal life. We can't remember what we did and what we were and the feelings we had. We know from the teachings of our prophets that we were faithful and trusted. Because we can remember only as far back as our mortal childhood, our Father in heaven knows us much better than we know ourselves. He knows our hearts and our minds. He knows what we really are and what we really want.

Because he knows the hearts and minds of all his children, he also knows those who can and will assist us in our eternal quest and those who would hinder us. He knows what will bring us the greatest ultimate fulfillment and how we can accomplish the greatest good in helping our brothers and sisters as we assist in building the kingdom of God. This guidance is free to all. The Lord is anxious to help all who will hear. (Revelation 3:13.) What may seem complex to us is not difficult to him. His thoughts are higher than ours, and his ways are higher than ours. His eternal vantage point permits him to see all things with an eternal perspective.

How foolish to leave the home of our Father, undertake a wonderful journey on this earth, and then refuse to invite him to give us direction throughout the journey!

Jesus Christ, the Son of God, taught the importance of prayer by word and deed. He also stressed the need to pray for specific things, and emphasized persistence in prayer.

Jesus, who exemplified the utmost love and respect for his Father in heaven, taught his disciples the importance of prayer, not by words alone, but also by his personal example.

When he went to the Jordan River to be baptized by John, he was thirty years of age and ready to represent his Father in a public ministry. Luke records the following about the baptism: "Now when all the people were baptized, it came to pass, that Jesus also being baptized, and praying, the heaven was opened." (Luke 3:21.)

Jesus felt deeply the need to communicate further with his Father, so he withdrew from the people and departed into the barren wilderness, where he fasted and communed with his Father for forty days. (Matthew 4:1-11.) He prayed when he was about to take any decisive step in his ministry. Before he selected the twelve apostles, "he went out into a mountain to pray, and continued all night in prayer to God." (Luke 6:12-13.) He often left his disciples so that he could communicate with his Father in heaven. Luke tells us: "And he withdrew himself into the wilderness, and prayed." (Luke 5:16.) Apparently he also prayed at the beginning of each day: "And in the morning, rising up a great while before day, he went out, and departed into a solitary place, and there prayed." (Mark 1:35.)

Jesus Christ has taught us to pray. Once when his disciples were with him as he prayed, they said, "Lord, teach us to pray." (Luke 11:1.) He responded to their request and taught them: "Our Father which art in heaven, Hallowed be thy name. Thy kingdom come. Thy will be done in earth, as it is in heaven. Give us this day our daily bread. And forgive us our debts, as we forgive our debtors. And lead us not into temptation, but deliver us from evil: For thine is the kingdom, and the power, and the glory for ever. Amen." (Matthew 6:9-13.)

This was a model prayer given to teach his followers

to pray individually, and from their hearts to praise and thank the Lord for his blessings to them. How uplifting, how refreshing, how revitalizing to pray in this manner as directed by our Lord Jesus Christ! Through focusing in prayer on the power, the majesty, the greatness and goodness of our Father in heaven, we are lifted above the pettiness and the frustrations of the moment and are praying for his kindness, his power, and his glory to advance here on the earth. At the conclusion of such a prayer perspective returns, and we can mentally and spiritually view the big picture, the things that really count.

We must beware lest our prayers become too self-centered. We must not let them lapse into asking nor be concerned only with our immediate personal desires so that our prayers focus only on ourselves and not on the Lord whom we are addressing. We need to be concerned about what we can do to make his name more hallowed on the earth. We need to be concerned about self-improvement so that through us his will may be done, and through our righteousness and unceasing efforts the power and glory of his kingdom can be advanced on the earth.

Our prayers are to be heart-expanding, mind-expanding, and soul-expanding through expressions of praise and thanksgiving to our Lord. They should lift us above the tiny universe that revolves around each of us to the magnificent kingdom of God and our part in it. We should come away from prayer refreshed and with our trust in him deepened, our gratitude increased, our vision broadened, and our resolves strengthened, refreshed, and invigorated as we turn to the tasks and opportunities at hand.

Paul admonishes all of us who put on the whole armor of God to continue "praying always." (Ephesians 6:18.) Jesus Christ emphasized repeatedly the need for persistence in prayer. He did not want his disciples to become discouraged or to give up. He wanted them to continue in prayer.

Immediately after the Savior gave his disciples the Lord's Prayer, he gave them a parable of the friend at midnight, which teaches the rewards of persistency:

> And he said unto them, Which of you shall have a friend, and shall go unto him at midnight, and say unto him, Friend, lend me three loaves;
> For a friend of mine in his journey is come to me, and I have nothing to set before him?
> And he from within shall answer and say, Trouble me not: the door is now shut, and my children are with me in bed; I cannot rise and give thee.
> I say unto you, Though he will not rise and give him, because he is his friend, yet because of his importunity he will rise and give him as many as he needeth. (Luke 11:5-8.)

Immediately after teaching this parable, Jesus said, "And I say unto you, Ask, and it shall be given you; seek, and ye shall find; knock, and it shall be opened unto you." (Luke 11:9.)

In Luke, Jesus reemphasized the importance of persisting in prayer. "And he spake a parable unto them to this end, that men ought always to pray, and not to faint." (Luke 18:1.) "Not to faint" means not to become faint-hearted or discouraged, but to continue seeking through prayer.

This same emphasis on persistence in prayer has continued in our day. In the Doctrine and Covenants, the Lord says: "Pray always, and I will pour out my Spirit upon you, and great shall be your blessing." (D&C 19:38.) "Pray always, that you may come off conqueror; yea, that you may conquer Satan." (D&C 10:5.) "Pray always, that ye may not faint." (D&C 88:126.) "Search diligently, pray always, and be believing, and all things shall work together for your good." (D&C 90:24.)

In September 1823, young Joseph Smith knelt in his room and continued in prayer persistently for a long time. Long after everyone else in the family had gone to sleep, he sought the Lord. Suddenly a light appeared in his room, "which continued to increase until the room was lighter than at noonday." The heavenly messenger spoke to Joseph and told him that his name was Moroni, that he was sent of God. Joseph Smith's humble, persistent prayer was answered. (Joseph Smith—History 29-33.)

President David O. McKay learned the value of persistence in prayer and persistence in patiently and effectively serving the Lord. He wrote:

> One day in my youth I was hunting cattle. While climbing a steep hill, I stopped to let my horse rest, and there, once again, an intense desire came over me to receive a manifestation of the truth of the restored gospel. I dismounted, threw my reins over my horse's head, and there under a serviceberry bush I prayed that God would declare to me the truth of his revelation to Joseph Smith. I am sure that I prayed fervently and sincerely and with as much faith as a young boy could muster.
>
> At the conclusion of the prayer, I arose from my knees, threw the reins over my faithful pony's head, and got into the saddle. As I started along the trail again, I remember saying to myself, "No spiritual manifestation has come to me. If I am true to myself I must say I am just the same 'old boy' that I was before I prayed."
>
> The Lord did not see fit to give me an answer on that occasion, but in 1899, after I had been appointed president of the Scottish Conference, the spiritual manifestation for which I had prayed as a boy in my teens came as a natural sequence to the performance of duty. (Claire Middlemiss, comp., *Cherished Experiences from the Writings of President David O. McKay* [Deseret Book, 1976 ed.], pp. 6-7.)

Alma, the great Book of Mormon prophet, taught his son Helaman:

> Yea, and cry unto God for all thy support; yea, let all thy doings be unto the Lord, and whithersoever thou goest let it be in the Lord; yea, let thy thoughts be directed unto the Lord; yea, let the affections of thy heart be placed upon the Lord forever.
>
> Counsel with the Lord in all thy doings, and he will direct thee for good; yea, when thou liest down at night lie down unto the Lord, that he may watch over you in your sleep; and when thou risest in the morning let thy heart be full of thanks unto God; and if ye do these things, ye shall be lifted up at the last day. (Alma 37:36-37.)

The Lord has told us he will give us grace sufficient for the day. We cannot pray on Sunday for the whole week, nor can we pray in January for the entire year, nor can we ask him to bless us in the preparation of all our family home evening lessons for the entire year. We pray for assistance in preparing each week's lesson and we ask his help in presenting it to our children. Then he gives us his help and power sufficient for the task. He has said, "But behold, I say unto you that ye must pray always, and not faint; that ye must not perform any thing unto the Lord save in the first place ye shall pray unto the Father in the name of Christ, that he will consecrate thy performance unto thee, that thy performance may be for the welfare of thy soul." (2 Nephi 32:9.)

To those who truly love the Lord, it is not a task to seek him, but a privilege that is sought gladly. It affords to those who love him the opportunity to express gratitude to him and humbly seek his guidance for the day and the task at hand.

Why is the Lord so concerned that we continue in prayer? that we persist in prayer? that we pray always? He has told us that he cannot bless us unless we fulfill the law that brings the blessing: "For all who will have a blessing at my hands shall abide the law which was appointed for that blessing, and the conditions thereof, as were instituted from before the foundation of the world." (D&C 132:5.) "There is a law irrevocably decreed in heaven before the foundations of this world, upon which all blessings are predicated—And when we obtain any blessing from God, it is by obedience to that law upon which it is predicated." (D&C 130:20-21.)

We may begin to seek a blessing from the Lord even when we do not have adequate faith or are not worthy, for by persisting in prayer and adding self-introspection, obedience, and repentance over a period of time, we can eventually fulfill the law and become worthy to receive the blessing we seek. It is the Lord who determines the blessing after we fulfill the law, and the eternal blessing may not always be the one that we desire at that particular moment in mortality.

Following is a touching story as told by President Heber J. Grant:

My wife Lucy was very sick for nearly three years prior to her death. At one time I was in the hospital with her for six months. When she was dying, I called my children into the bedroom and told them their mamma was dying. My daughter Lutie said she did not want her mamma to die, and insisted that I lay hands upon her and heal her, saying that she had often seen her mother, when sick in the hospital, in San Francisco, suffering intensely, go to sleep immediately and have a peaceful night's rest, when I had blessed her. I explained to my children that we all had to die, some time, and that I felt that their mamma's time had come. The children went out of the room, and I knelt down by the bed of my dying wife, and told the Lord that I acknowledged his hand in life or in death, in joy or in sorrow, in prosperity or adversity; that I did not complain because my wife was dying, but that I lacked the strength to see my wife die and have her death affect the faith of my children in the ordinances of the gospel. I therefore pleaded with him to give to my daughter Lutie a testimony that it was his will that her mother should die. Within a few short hours, my wife breathed her last. Then I called the children into the bedroom and announced that their mamma was dead. My little boy, Heber, commenced weeping bitterly, and Lutie put her arms around him and kissed him, and told him not to cry, that the voice of the Lord had said to her, "In the death of your mamma the will of the Lord will be done." Lutie knew nothing of my prayers, and this manifestation to her was a direct answer to my supplication to the Lord, and for it I have never ceased to be grateful. (*Improvement Era,* June 1912, pp. 726-27.)

There are times when God in his infinite wisdom cannot grant that which we desire, but we should still, as his children, express our gratitude to him for our very existence. To seek him and express gratitude unto him only when things go our way is unbecoming to a child of God. We should honor him in bad times as well as good, in times of suffering as well as in times of health, in grief as well as in happiness.

President Grant exemplifies this spirit of meekness, of submissiveness, for although God did not grant his beloved wife's life, he could speak comfort to his grieving, questioning daughter. How foolish it would be to shut ourselves off from a concerned, loving God if things did not happen just as we had requested!

We, above all people on the earth, are blessed with a true knowledge of God. We know that he has a body of flesh and bone, that Jesus Christ does also, and that the Holy Ghost is a personage of Spirit. We know of the tender love of God for each of his children. Because we are his children and he cares for us, we should persistently pray for specific blessings and return to him and thank him in specific terms.

Apparently Jesus did not pray in generalities as we sometimes do. He prayed specifically for the things he needed to give strength and bring success in his daily activities. His Father was not distant; rather, he was real and close. Always after receiving specific blessings, our Lord returned and thanked his Father for the blessings he had received.

An example of praying specifically is found in the life of Parley P. Pratt. In the early days of the Church, Elder Pratt was called to undertake a mission to Canada. Following is his own account:

> I took leave and entered Hamilton, a flourishing town at the head of Lake Ontario; but my place of destination was Toronto, around on the north side of the lake. If I went by land I would have a circuitous route, muddy and tedious to go on foot. The lake had just opened, and steamers had commenced plying between the two places; two dollars would convey me to Toronto in a few hours, and save days of laborious walking; but I was an entire stranger in Hamilton, and also in the province; and money I had none. Under these circumstances I pondered what I should do. I had many times received answers to prayer in such matters; but now it seemed hard to exercise faith, because I was among strangers and entirely unknown. The Spirit seemed to whisper to me to try the Lord, and see if anything was too hard for him, that I might know and trust Him under all circumstances. I retired to a secret place in a forest and prayed to the Lord for money to enable me to cross the lake. I then entered Hamilton and commenced to chat with some of the people. I had not tarried many minutes before I was accosted by a stranger, who inquired my name and where I was going. He also asked me if I did not want some money. I said yes. He then gave me ten dollars and a letter of introduction to John Taylor. . . . (*Autobiography of Parley P. Pratt* [Deseret Book, 1964], pp. 134-35.)

101

Money and a letter of introduction to John Taylor—
what a remarkable answer to prayer! John Taylor, who
became the third president of the Church, was baptized
by Elder Pratt, as were many others. The same power of
prayer that existed during the time of the Lord Jesus
Christ, of Paul, of Joseph Smith, and of Parley P. Pratt
and John Taylor continues today.

President John Taylor has taught us to follow the
influence of the Spirit of the Lord:

There is quite a fine opportunity now for men—good men,
pure and virtuous men and women to raise up a goodly seed. . . . As
things progress get better houses and better gardens and surround-
ings in keeping with them. And upon everything we do we need the
blessing of the Almighty; and we need to put our trust in him. If,
for instance, I was living here and was raising a family, the first
thing which I should do would be to dedicate myself and my
family, my house and garden, my land, my cattle, and everything I
possessed to God, and should ask his blessing upon them. Then
every morning when I arose I should kneel down to supplicate his
blessing upon me and mine during the day, to preserve us from evil
influences, accidents and dangers, and to otherwise bless our labors
in obtaining a livelihood. And then I would pray for those who
presided over me in the Priesthood. Joseph Smith, upwards of forty
years ago, said to me: Brother Taylor, you have received the Holy
Ghost. Now follow the influence of that Spirit, and it will lead you
into all truth, until by and by, it will become in you a principle of
revelation. Then he told me never to arise in the morning without
bowing before the Lord, and dedicating myself to him during that
day. Some people treat these things lightly. I do not; because I
know that we derive our food, our raiment, and all earthly as well
as spiritual blessings from the goodness of God our Heavenly
Father. I know, furthermore, that as President of this Church I
should not know how to dictate if the Lord did not help me. Should
I desire people to yield to my ideas? I have ~~ ideas only as God
gives them to me. . . . I have a desire, when a 'hing comes along,
to learn the will of God, and then to do it, and t 'each my brethren
to do it, that we may all grow up unto Christ o ' living head, that
we may be acquainted with correct principles an govern ourselves
accordingly. . . . The scriptures tell us that he th hath eternal life
is rich; and the Lord has told us to seek after tl e riches of eternal
life. (*Journal of Discourses* 22:313-14.)

Each of us needs the Lord's guidance, and we receive it as we pray worthily.

Three verses of modern-day scripture are particularly helpful in understanding how the Lord answers prayers and guides us here on this earth. All were given through Joseph Smith the Prophet to Oliver Cowdery. They are:

1. "Verily, verily, I say unto you, if you desire a further witness, cast your mind upon the night that you cried unto me in your heart, that you might know concerning the truth of these things. Did I not speak peace to your mind concerning the matter? What greater witness can you have than from God?" (D&C 6:22-23.)

Oliver had had some doubts in his mind, and the Lord through Joseph Smith told him to cast his thoughts back on the night that he sought Him in his heart. Did not the Lord speak to his mind? What greater witness can one have than from God! Man or man's imagination is not capable of creating that kind of witness which is characterized by peace that passeth understanding, a burning in the bosom.

2. The second revelation was given when Oliver desired to have the gift of revelation. The Lord said:

"Yea, behold, I will tell you in your mind and in your heart, by the Holy Ghost, which shall come upon you and which shall dwell in your heart. Now, behold, this is the spirit of revelation; behold, this is the spirit by which Moses brought the children of Israel through the Red Sea on dry ground." (D&C 8:2-3.)

3. The third scripture is one that is well known and oft quoted. Oliver attempted to translate but without success. Through the Prophet Joseph Smith, these words were given to him:

"Behold, you have not understood; you have supposed that I would give it unto you, when you took no thought save it was to ask me.

"But, behold, I say unto you, that you must study it out in your mind; then you must ask me if it be right, and if it is right I will cause that your bosom shall burn within you; therefore, you shall feel that it is right.

"But if it be not right you shall have no such feelings, but you shall have a stupor of thought that shall cause you to forget the thing which is wrong; therefore, you cannot write that which is sacred save it be given you from me." (D&C 9:7-9.)

The Lord, who is kind and gentle, sometimes communicates to us with a still (subdued, serene, calm) small voice. He desires to protect and enhance our free agency, while Satan, our adversary, doesn't respect free agency, but would destroy it through appeals to pride, vanity, lust, envy, hatred, and desire for power.

President Brigham Young counseled his son Brigham Young, Jr., how to pray. In these helpful instructions we learn better how to pray with the help of the Spirit of the Lord:

> In 1864, he [Brigham Young, Jr.] returned to Europe, to assist President Daniel H. Wells in the presidency of the European mission. Before leaving home, President Young took his son aside and said to him: "My son, you are going away upon a long and important mission. You will have heavy responsibility placed upon you, and you will not be near me so as to receive help and counsel. But there is One always near you, who will listen to your prayer and give you counsel and help. Whenever you are in doubt or trouble, go to Him in secret, and state your case fully to Him just as you would to me. He knows your desire, but there is a power in expressed or uttered prayer. You may not understand or desire the best way, and if you put your thoughts into words, the Spirit will make things plain to your mind, and teach you through your own words exactly what to pray for. Therefore, just talk to the Lord, and explain fully what you want. It is your right to receive revelation, and God will give it unto you just when and how you need it. When you seek Him you will find Him. (Susa Young Gates, "Lives of Our Leaders, the Apostles," *Juvenile Instructor,* May 1, 1900, pp. 262-63.)

Through an angel the Lord emphasized another aspect of prayer: ". . . and be agreed as touching all things whatsoever ye ask of me. . . ." (D&C 27:18.) This is a plea for unity in the things we ask of God. We are to be united in the Church and in our families. The Lord has said, "Be one; and if ye are not one ye are not mine." (D&C 38:27.) Then, when we are united, or unified, we should seek the Lord's blessings. There is power in reaching an agreement or desiring an agreement, being united, being as one, and petitioning the Lord.

We should thank the Lord and praise him that we live on the earth when the whole armor of God is available and that we can have the great blessing of putting it on. Then, when we petition the Lord in prayer, he will help us keep the armor on and bless us to use it properly and receive the resultant blessings.

Chapter 10

WATCHING WITH ALL PERSEVERANCE

*. . . and watching thereunto
with all perseverance and supplication
for all saints. (Ephesians 6:18.)
. . . let my army become very great, and let it be
sanctified before me
that it may be come fair as the sun, and clear as
the moon. . . . (D&C 105:31.)*

We are not isolated soldiers fighting evil individually. We are part of a vast army that is ever increasing in skill, ability, and righteousness as well as in numbers. Each soldier has his specific duties, none of which may be overlooked or done halfheartedly, for that will not only reflect upon the entire army, but it will also weaken the entire army.

Each soldier has a responsibility to his fellow soldiers and to his officers. He must know his duty and act with diligence. "Wherefore, now let every man learn his duty, and to act in the office in which he is appointed, in all diligence. He that is slothful shall not be counted worthy to stand, and he that learns not his duty and shows himself not approved shall not be counted worthy to stand. . . ." (D&C 107:99-100.)

"Worthy" means meritorious or exemplary. "Stand" means to remain firm or steadfast, as in a cause.

The Lord's army is the sum total of all of the individual members. Just as there can be no army without soldiers, so there can be no church without members. There is no disciplined army without disciplined soldiers, no outstanding church without outstanding members. Great officers are essential, vital, and a blessing to a great army, but officers, no matter how great, do not and cannot constitute an entire army; there must be those in the ranks who may not be highly visible, but who are dependable and capable.

The Lord referred to his army as being very large and terrible to the wicked. The leader of the army is our Lord Jesus Christ.

"Fair as the sun" means "beautiful, able to see clearly." "Clear" is like a light in the darkness—truth and light, dispelling falsehood, error, darkness, fear, and evil.

A sanctified army is filled with light and truth that are "terrible" to the evil because darkness cannot withstand light. Darkness must give way, error and falsehood must flee when confronted by truth.

Each soldier who makes up the Lord's army has a great individual responsibility. He may be a worthy, contributing member or he may be a detriment to it. Each one must eventually either improve or cease to be a part of the great army of the latter days. We can't live in a vacuum, thinking only of ourselves. We must wake up, prepare, and act. We must be capable and willing to fill an important role in the Lord's great army.

In war, especially against an enemy who is without honor and is totally unscrupulous, we must continually assist each other if we are to succeed. How heartless it would be for a soldier to look at a fellow soldier who was fighting for his life surrounded by the enemy and say, "I expected it. He had it coming. It's his fault. It serves him right." It is almost unthinkable that a soldier in God's army would be so insensitive and unfeeling as to take pleasure in another's misfortune, regardless of who caused the misfortune. If a fellow soldier becomes surrounded by evil isolated from good, we should rush to his defense and throw ourselves into the battle to save him.

It would also be unthinkable for us to stand by analyzing a situation and arriving at a conclusion as to why it happened, and then let such knowledge satisfy us to the point that we let another person be destroyed because we know why it is happening. No matter what the cause or whose fault, we must assist. If any person is destroyed, regardless of the reason, he is still destroyed.

During wartime several years ago, a Latter-day Saint couple were driving down a street in a large city and noticed a young serviceman in the clutches of an undesirable woman. She was trying to persuade him to enter an apartment building with her. The couple did not just shake their heads in disgust or outrage; they stopped the car, walked over, and asked the serviceman if they could give him a ride to camp or some other place he might desire to go. The woman was enraged, but the young man accepted the invitation of the interested couple. They became friends, and when they parted, he took their names and address. A few days later the couple received a letter from the young serviceman's mother. She expressed her gratitude and said that as nearly as she could determine, at the very time that they were intervening and rescuing her son, she was on her knees praying that he would come home to her morally clean. This couple did not pass by, thinking it was just another case of a lonely, homesick serviceman and an evil woman. They fought for him, a stranger, and won.

The Lord has given to us in our scriptures a superb example of commitment to others—the example of the sons of Mosiah. With the Spirit of the Lord working with them, their thoughts were directed to the Lamanites. (Mosiah 28:3-7.) Each of the sons of Mosiah rejected the opportunity to be king in order to become a missionary to the Lamanites. The Lamanites had never known anyone who served the Lord Jesus Christ, so the sons of Mosiah had to show them what it meant to be committed to Jesus Christ. Over a period of years among the Lamanites, the sons of Mosiah returned good for evil and love for hate. Their example eventually brought them amazing success. Ammon summarized their success in the following way:

And now behold, we have come, and been forth amongst them; and we have been patient in our sufferings, and we have suffered every privation; . . .

And we have entered into their houses and taught them, and we have taught them in their streets; yea, and we have taught them upon their hills; and we have also entered into their temples and their synagogues and taught them; and we have been cast out, and mocked, and spit upon, and smote upon our cheeks; and we have been stoned, and taken and bound with strong cords, and cast into prison; and through the power and wisdom of God we have been delivered again.

And we have suffered all manner of afflictions, and all this, that perhaps we might be the means of saving some soul; and we supposed that our joy would be full if perhaps we could be the means of saving some.

· Now behold, we can look forth and see the fruits of our labors; and are they few? I say unto you, Nay, they are many; yea, and we can witness of their sincerity, because of their love towards their brethren and also towards us. (Alma 26:28-31.)

There never were people like these among the descendants of Lehi. This was not just Ammon's opinion of these converts; it became obvious to all as the sons of Mosiah led their thousands of brothers and sisters back to the land of the Nephites. Perhaps the question "what if" could appropriately be asked. What if the sons of Mosiah had not been committed? What if the sons of Mosiah had taken only the easy course? There would have been thousands, tens of thousands who would never have known God. A great work for the Lord would never have been performed.

This attitude of commitment is as obvious in the life of Alma as it is in the lives of the sons of Mosiah. Alma led a group of missionaries to reclaim the Zoramites who had apostatized. Their apostasy was evidenced by their manner of worship. They had built a high platform in the center of their synagogue, and they mounted that platform, one at a time, on their day of worship; then each individual offered "the self-same prayer." The prayer, in essence, was "Lord, I thank thee that I am more outstanding than others. Let us keep it that way. Amen." Alma was astonished when he observed their exceeding pride. He counted the cost in advance. He knew that he and his fellow missionaries would be persecuted; however, it apparently never entered his mind to shirk from the task at hand because of the difficulty of the assignment. He knelt down and prayed to the Lord:

> O Lord, my heart is exceeding sorrowful; wilt thou comfort my soul in Christ. O Lord, wilt thou grant unto me that I may have strength, that I may suffer with patience these afflictions which shall come upon me, because of the iniquity of this people. . .
>
> Wilt thou grant unto them [his co-laborers] that they may have strength, that they may bear their afflictions which shall come upon them because of the iniquities of this people.
>
> O Lord, wilt thou grant unto us that we may have success in bringing them again unto thee in Christ.
>
> Behold, O Lord, their souls are precious, and many of them are our brethren; therefore, give unto us, O Lord, power and wisdom that we may bring these, our brethren, again unto thee. (Alma 31:31, 33-35.)

After uttering this humble and fervent prayer, Alma blessed his companions that they would be strengthened by the Lord and, despite persecution, would be able to gain success and joy in their labors. Their assignment was not convenient; it called for commitment. They were willing to serve with all their heart, might, mind, and strength. It is obvious that the Lord is well pleased with those who will put him first in their lives—those who serve not just when it is convenient, but also when it is inconvenient.

The souls in our home, our Primary class, our Sunday School class, our seminary class are every bit as precious in God's sight as the souls of the Lamanites or the Zoramites, and we may have to work as hard to save them.

Recently as I was walking down a hall in our meetinghouse I saw a man pressing a lesson manual into the hands of a Sunday School president. As I passed I heard him say: "I've taught that class two weeks and if they don't care for me, then I'm not going back. Get someone else."

I thought of the sons of Mosiah. It took years for them to save souls. It took years to show a better way of life by their example. They returned good for evil, love for hate, kindness for unkindness. Finally some who had been the very most hardhearted were touched by the Spirit and came to God. How will those who need help ever learn if they are not taught and led by dedicated Latter-day Saints who are committed followers of the Lord Jesus Christ?

We need servants of God who, to save souls, will not only absorb some unpleasantness but even pain, if necessary.

Can we reflect on our Savior in Gethsemane and think of him on the cross and still give but little to those who need so much? Can we really reflect upon how much we have because of the sacrifice of others in the past as well as those in the present and sleep soundly without first giving thanks?

If we are giving less than our all, then we ought to be embarrassed, considering the covenants we have made.

> . . . and now, as ye are desirous to come into the fold of God, and to be called his people, and are willing to bear one another's burdens, that they may be light;
> Yea, and are willing to mourn with those that mourn; yea, and comfort those that stand in need of comfort, and to stand as witnesses of God at all times and in all things, and in all places that ye may be in, even until death, that ye may be redeemed of God, and be numbered with those of the first resurrection, that ye may have eternal life—

Now I say unto you, if this be the desire of your hearts, what have you against being baptized in the name of the Lord, as a witness before him that ye have entered into a covenant with him, that ye will serve him and keep his commandments, that he may pour out his Spirit more abundantly upon you? (Mosiah 18:8-10.)

This is the key not only to building and sustaining the kingdom of God, but also to success and and happiness in this life. "He that loseth his life for my sake shall find it," the Savior said. (Matthew 10:39.)

How easy it is to walk the extra mile helping someone who has been injured. We can completely forget our own efforts as we become caught up in the well-being of the one we are assisting. We are there because he is there, and we remember little of our own inconvenience or fatigue.

How fascinating and interesting is the battle when we are more concerned about our brothers and sisters, our fellow soldiers and their welfare, than about ourselves and our own welfare. A personal wound may seem a small thing if we are struggling to protect and save a fallen friend. How little attention we give to our own bruises if we are attending to the bruises of another. We are dependent upon each other. We need each other. We have promised that we will bear one another's burdens that they may be light, and mourn with and comfort those that mourn and those who are in need of comfort. When we can see only our own burdens, they become magnified and overwhelm us. When we cease mourning for others and mourn for ourselves, we are overwhelmed by self-pity and there is no comfort for us; we cannot comfort others. We become effective soldiers only by losing ourselves in thinking, caring, and acting in behalf of others.

If an army has numerous soldiers who are well trained and strong, the chances of an individual soldier's not only surviving but being triumphant are much greater than if the army is small, poorly trained, and weak. We, of course, seek to encourage and protect our fellow soldiers because we love them and desire their safety. However, we benefit greatly individually if the army remains strong. When we save a brother or sister we increase our own chances of victory over the enemy. The following personal experience illustrates this point.

I labored many months to bring a capable young institute student to a knowledge of the gospel. Then he was called on a mission. One day several months later a series of things happened that brought me to a position of feeling unsuccessful, unhappy, and discouraged. Then a letter arrived from my young missionary friend. He wrote: "Dear Brother Hartshorn: I don't know if you ever get discouraged, but if you do, here are some things I want you to know. . . ."

He then told me of the goodness of the Lord to him. He told me of many convert baptisms. He bore his testimony and closed by expressing his appreciation to me for my contribution to his life. As I laid the letter aside, I realized something wonderful had taken place inside me. I felt peaceful and happy; all discouragement had vanished. I was refreshed, strengthened, and ready to move forward in the Lord's work.

We cannot bless the lives of others without our own lives being blessed. This is especially true when it applies to members of our own family. We cannot strengthen others without strength flowing back to us. "Therefore, strengthen your brethren in all your conversation, in all your prayers, in all your exhortations, and in all your doing." (D&C 108:7.)

The Savior suffered, bled, and died for all who would accept his infinite sacrifice. There was no selecting process on his part. He prepared the way and invited all to enter. He rejoices over all who follow him and weeps over those who refuse.

We must beware that we do not exclude any from our association and friendship because of personality, disposition, or something else that we may dislike. We are not members of a church and kingdom that withholds from anyone. In the Book of Mormon we read:

> Behold, hath he commanded any that they should depart out of the synagogues, or out of the houses of worship? Behold, I say unto you, Nay.
>
> Hath he commanded any that they should not partake of his salvation? Behold I say unto you, Nay; but he hath given it free for all men; and he hath commanded his people that they should persuade all men to repentance.
>
> Behold, hath the Lord commanded any that they should not partake of his goodness? Behold I say unto you, Nay; but all men are privileged the one like unto the other, and none are forbidden. (2 Nephi 26:26-28.)

As servants of our Lord Jesus Christ, we are to follow his example. If there are those whom we do not care for, then the second principle of the gospel should be applied in our lives. We know how to repent; we do not have to continue thoughts or behavior that is hurtful to others and detrimental to ourselves. In the end, the one who shuns will be hurt more than the one who is shunned.

How is it possible that a person who knows the bruises and the fatigue of battle can be unsympathetic, perhaps even unfeeling, when another person is distressed? We are one. We truly are a part of God's army. We must not only look the part but also *be* a part.

We have a living prophet to guide us today. We follow his leadership. Joseph Smith led with inspiration, courage, and vigor in his day and we are blessed recipients of the inspired scripture that came through him. But our present prophet is now chosen of God and leads us as his spokesman in this day. We joyfully follow him, for we cannot be God's army unless we are united under the leadership of our prophet. An army that ignores commands and directions ceases to be an army and becomes an undisciplined, uncoordinated, unruly group.

How confusing and detrimental it would be to the Lord's work if the words from our mouths were contrary to the words from the mouth of the prophet of God! If this happened out of malice or ignorance, the effect would be detrimental to the progress of God's work on the earth. We must be humble enough and diligent enough not to let this happen, so that honest seekers are not confused and the work of the Lord is not held back. May I share a personal example, a time of decision in my life.

It was a Sabbath morning, when I was nearly nineteen years of age. I had arisen early, attended priesthood meeting, and had returned home to await the beginning of Sunday School. I sat down on the front lawn. I had some thinking to do, some questions to resolve. I began a conversation with myself. "Do you want to serve the Lord?" I asked. "Do you want to commit yourself to his way of life—throughout your whole life? What kind of a person do you want to marry? Do you really want to be married in the temple? What kind of a husband do you want to be? What kind of a father do you want to be?" And then a question that demanded an almost immediate answer: "What will you say if the bishop asks you to go on a mission?" I had asked myself these questions—questions ever so important. I didn't have the answers.

Our family home was half a block from the ward chapel, and nearly everyone walked to meetings. As I sat pondering, my neighbors walked by and waved or called out pleasant greetings.

I found a quiet place and prayed, then joined my friends and neighbors at Sunday School, followed by fast and testimony meeting. I sat in deep meditation. I had asked the questions, but I still did not have the answers.

It seems that some are affected by one lesson, one thought, one teacher, and others by an accumulation of lessons, thoughts, and the examples of many teachers. There is usually nothing spectacular about the latter process. Growth is slow, almost imperceptible; I suppose it might be discouraging to those who are not committed to the Lord.

On that particular day of decision in my life those who were committed and had persisted were seated about me. I turned and momentarily studied several of them.

There was Brother Liebelt. He had lived in Germany in his younger years and whenever he wanted to visit the families assigned to him by his branch president, he had to walk forty miles. He had continued to carry out every church assignment with the same tenacity, and he expected this kind of commitment from others. And Brother Hoglund. He was Swedish, and proud of it. His laugh would warm any heart, and one would not be in his presence long without hearing his laugh. Brother Sorensen was a big man who spoke with a drawl and always knew a humorous story. Brother Sorensen and young people went together; when you saw him, you also saw a group of teenagers. There was Brother Steiner in the same place; I couldn't remember when I hadn't seen him there, his family with him, a quiet man. More than anything else, doing the right thing, being in the right place at the right time, bespoke his conviction.

Testimony bearing had commenced now and one of the first to stand was Brother Proctor. This was not unusual. No one questioned his sincerity as he bore his witness to the truth of the gospel. As the meeting progressed the others whom I had been looking at stood and bore witness also. They hadn't sought for personal recognition; it seemed that they were part of a cooperative effort to do good through teaching, leading, and guiding.

I had asked myself questions and now I had answers. "If that's what living the gospel does, if living the gospel will make me like they are, if it will make me like my neighbors, then I want to commit myself to the Lord Jesus Christ. That's the kind of life I want."

I felt the Spirit as I had never felt it before. I stood and said words that I had never spoken before, words that I have since spoken hundreds of times in hundreds of different places. I said: "I know that Jesus is the Christ. I know that the gospel is true. I know that Joseph Smith is a prophet of God, and I know that we have a living prophet at the head of this church today." I then added, "I want to thank all of you for what you've done for me. I want to go on a mission."

The decision had been made; the course my life would take had been determined, not as a result of any one lesson or any one teacher, but because of the continual example of many who seemed always to be concerned with me as an individual.

The Lord has said: "And if it so be that you should labor all your days . . . and bring, save it be one soul unto me, how great shall be your joy in the kingdom of my Father!" (D&C 18:15.) Yes, and how great shall be the joy of the one who is brought to the Lord!

I am grateful to those who watched me, assisted me, and taught me with perseverance and supplication. Then I could see the good fruits of the gospel in their lives, and now I have them in my life. May we all watch with all perseverance and supplication for all saints, as the Lord has told us.

Chapter 11

AND HAVING DONE ALL, STAND

. . . and having done all, to stand.
(Ephesians 6:13.)
. . . having done all, that ye may be able
to stand. (D&C 27:15.)

"Having done all" means that the individual has put on the whole armor of God, is praying always, and is watching with all perseverance. Such an individual is then admonished to stand against evil, battle continuously, and not fall. He must stand in purity and in righteousness, defending and advancing the great cause of the Lord Jesus Christ.

Some Latter-day Saints wrongly suppose that a time will come when they can relax, lay the shield and the sword aside, and look back on past victories. That does not happen in this life. Some persons, when the looked-for and longed-for respite does not materialize, become disheartened, discouraged, and even bitter. But the enemy is always awaiting with anticipation a moment when we are less than vigilant, less than prepared for the battle. He attacks at any time, in any way, and in any place he can to obtain an advantage. The attack may be subtle or it may be obvious. He and his followers and their converts to evil are the enemies of God and his righteousness and of his righteous people.

If Satan continues to attack and we have no rest (as the world defines rest), that is not the Lord's doing. Satan chose to be as he is and his followers chose to be as they are. We must continue to advance with all possible care as well as with all speed in this life, to the instant that we draw our very last breath. We do not look for, plan for, anticipate, or expect a respite from the great battle for men's souls nor from the battle to secure this earth for the Lord and his devoted followers, that glorious time when all who are faithful will be completely free from the influence of evil.

The well-equipped, powerful, dependable, skilled soldier will find himself more and more where the battle is raging because he *is* well equipped.

Should it be surprising that we encounter opposition, when the Lord has told us we are at war and we are dressed in the armor of war? Should it be surprising that he would use well-trained, valuable soldiers continually? No. It *would* be surprising if the Lord's soldiers found themselves on extended furloughs while the battle raged and spiritual lives were endangered. If this simple truth is overlooked or forgotten, we could become discouraged.

The soldier in battle may take stunning blows and experience cuts and bruises, hunger, thirst, and fatigue, yet triumph. Because we in this life do battle, we also experience the consequences of battle.

Paul wrote to the Corinthians: "We are troubled on every side, yet not distressed; we are perplexed, but not in despair; Persecuted, but not forsaken; cast down, but not destroyed." (2 Corinthians 4:8-9.)

This courageous attitude is evident in all the valiant soldiers of God in this dispensation. The Prophet Joseph Smith said: "If I were sunk into the lowest pit of Nova Scotia, with the Rocky Mountains piled on me, I would hang on, exercise faith, and keep up good courage, and I would come out on top." (John Henry Evans, *Joseph Smith, An American Prophet* [Deseret Book, 1966], p. 9.)

In a letter to John Smith, the Prophet said: ". . . I write these few lines to inform you that we feel determined in this place not to be dismayed if hell boils over all at once. We feel to hope for the best, and determined to prepare for the worst." (*History of the Church* 6:485-86.)

The angel told the Prophet Joseph Smith, "Lift up your hearts and rejoice, . . . and take upon you my whole armor." (D&C 27:15.) Why should putting on the whole armor of God cause one to rejoice and be joyful? The whole armor of God can be put on only when the whole armor is available on the earth. During many centuries of the earth's existence, it was not available because of the absence of the gospel from the earth. So after hundreds of years the angel says "rejoice"—rejoice in the magnificent opportunity you have because now the armor is once again available—not the armor of man, but of God. We rejoice because we know that we may be protected by God's whole armor every step of our earthly journey.

Jedediah M. Grant, a zealous servant of God and counselor to Brigham Young, said the following, from which we learn that those in the forefront of the battle are happy, while those who seek happiness where all is calm and undisturbed will be seeking happiness where it cannot be found:

> In order to understand the principle of happiness you must not be ever complaining, but learn not to fret yourselves. If things do not go right, let them go as they will, if they go rough, let it be so; if all hell boils over, let it boil. I thank the Lord for the bitter as well as for the sweet; I like to grapple with the opposite: I like to work and have something to oppose. I used to dread those things, but now I like to grapple with opposition, and there is plenty of it on the right hand and on the left. When trouble gets in among you, shake it off, or bid it stand out of the way. If the devil should come and say, "Brother Brigham is not doing his duty, or is not doing

right," kick him right out of your way; bid him depart, do not allow him to have place in your habitation, but learn to be happy. . . .

How is it that brother Brigham is able to comfort and soothe those who are depressed in spirit, and always make those with whom he associates so happy? I will tell you . . . the man who is happy himself can make others feel so, for the light of God is in him, and others feel happy in his society. (*Journal of Discourses* 3:11.)

Brigham Young also commented on happiness: "There is not that man or woman in this congregation, or on the face of the earth, that has the privilege of the holy Gospel, and lives strictly to it, whom all hell can make unhappy. You cannot make the man, woman, or child unhappy, who possesses the Spirit of the living God; unhappiness is caused by some other spirit." (*Journal of Discourses* 3:343.)

Elder Parley P. Pratt, a dynamic servant of God, expressed his burning desire to serve God as follows:

If I had been set to turn the world over, to dig down a mountain, to go to the ends of the earth, or traverse the deserts of Arabia, it would have been easier than to have undertaken to rest, while the Priesthood was upon me. I have received the holy anointing, and I can never rest till the last enemy is conquered, death destroyed, and truth reigns triumphant. (*Journal of Discourses* 1:15.)

We all want to be strong, valiant, and righteous. Let us consider the following counsel from Brigham Young, who has given us an important key as to how we can be stronger:

What hinders this people from being as holy as the Church of Enoch? I can tell you the reason in a few words. It is because you will not cultivate the disposition to be so—*this comprehends the whole.* If my heart is not fully given up to this work, I will give my time, my talents, my hands, and my possessions to it, until my heart consents to be subject; I will make my hands labour in the cause of God until my heart bows in submission to it. . . .

Do you love the cause? "Yes," every heart at once responds, "I love the cause, I love the Lord and my religion." (*Journal of Discourses* 1:202, 216.)

Sometimes the cunning enemy whispers in our ear

with effective, continuing propaganda warfare designed to demoralize us. Satan whispers "the armor is grievous to bear; free yourself from it." Unless we are alert and understand our enemy, we may have a tendency to think we are put upon to be wearing the armor; we may call attention to the armor we wear, and how burdensome it is, and how very heroic we are for wearing it. If we begin to feel this way, Satan's insidious propaganda has already had a serious influence upon our lives.

A soldier who thinks it is a burden to wear God's armor will also think that he has been put upon by being recruited for God's army. He who proclaims such a false conception is a serious threat to the success of the Lord's army. Such an ungrateful soldier is a source of excuses to others who also have a tendency to be weak. He cannot be depended upon in time of battle, because he may well determine at a critical moment that it is not worth the effort, or he may join the enemy and ridicule the faithful. Such a soldier demands the attention of his fellow soldiers, who must expend effort unceasingly in an effort to convince him of the blessedness of his opportunity. A true soldier must have dignity. He must always maintain a humble feeling of his blessed privilege of being a part of the great king's army. His breastplate is to protect his heart. If his heart is right, he will be grateful for the privilege of serving.

Satan doesn't want his intended victims to recognize a test as a test. If a person were to come to the realization that he was actually in grave spiritual danger, he might arouse himself to a successful defense. But when he is unaware that he is approaching or passing through one of the battles of his life, he may be defeated so subtly that he doesn't even unsheath his sword. He may well be overcome and not know how it happened.

Some continually scan the horizon for any sign of an approaching enemy. This practice is commendable, provided, of course, that they are alert to a possible disguised enemy already in camp. Many who go astray do not go astray in the companionship of a clearly distinguishable enemy. Rather they are led astray in the company of so-called friends. They may falsely reason that if it is all right for fellow soldiers to act in a certain way, then it must not be *too* wrong. How tragic to rationalize oneself into sin!

Others are caught off guard because they are always looking to the future, looking to prepare for the big battle—the far-away mission, going away to school, a possible responsible position, a great test of poverty, a serious illness, or intense persecution. Such individuals fail to perceive that they are already in the heat of battle. The enemy is subtle, cunning, and deceitful. While they are watching and waiting for the big things, it may well be the little things that defeat them.

If we are to successfully combat evil, we must be constantly alert to what is really going on. We cannot afford to compromise or to rationalize. Satan will continue his cunning game; he will always say, "I am no devil and there is no hell," from one generation to the next, and carefully lead the souls of the unwary down to hell.

Satan varies his attack and we can't always know just what temptation or tactic he is going to use next, but the armor is exactly the same for each weapon used against us; the armor is exactly the same for each attack.

The armor that protects us against alcohol and tobacco is the same armor that protects us against adultery and all other moral violations. The armor that protects us against pride and vanity is the same armor that protects us against lying and stealing. Our coat of armor protects us against a multitude of sins and an unlimited number of attacks ranging from violent frontal attacks to subtle means. Some attacks may be avoided altogether because of the obvious preparation of the soldier.

The enemy won't waste his time attacking an armored soldier in the manner that he might attack an unarmored or partially armored individual. Wearing the whole armor of God always, with vigilance, is the price for success.

How wonderful it would be, as troops are deployed on the field of battle, if the leader could have a feeling of confidence knowing that *each* soldier knew his duty well and could be depended on. How many times does a valiant soldier have to ask what to do? How many times must one hear the same instructions? How many times does one have to be praised for doing things he has done before? Cannot the veteran soldier perform every task in an excellent manner? At each new opportunity, can he not know the mind of the Lord and proceed with confidence? Can he not perform a difficult task without receiving special praise and recognition? Is not the task well-performed and the contribution made a sufficient reward?

A young son must be praised much by his father so that he will not get discouraged and falter. A more mature son is not loved less by his father, for the years have brought a closeness and deepened appreciation; yet the father may speak less of his accomplishments, and that is the supreme compliment. How wonderful it is to be trusted implicitly!

God has called us to put his whole armor on and to become part of his royal army of the last days. It is a royal army because it is led by our Lord and King Jesus Christ. We often sing in our worship services:

Behold! a royal army, With banner, sword and shield,
Is marching forth to conquer, On life's great battlefield;
Its ranks are filled with soldiers, United, bold and strong,
Who follow their Commander, And sing their joyful song.

And now the foe advancing, That valiant host assails,
And yet they never falter; Their courage never fails;

Their Leader calls, "Be faithful!" They pass the word
*   along;*
They see his signal flashing, And shout their joyful song.

Oh, when the war is ended, When strife and conflicts
*   cease,*
When all are safely gathered Within the vale of peace,
Before the King eternal, That vast and mighty throng
Shall praise his name forever, And this shall be their
*   song:*

Victory, victory, Through him that redeemed us!
Victory, victory, Through Jesus Christ our Lord!
Victory, victory, victory, Through Jesus Christ our Lord!

—Hymns, no. 7

We are the children of God. We are meant to be dressed in shining armor, we move ever forward with dignity and honor in the army of our Lord. That is our commission, our calling. We are the hope of the world. Let us joyfully march forth. There should be no complaining, for we are soldiers in a royal army.

If we want ultimate peace and ultimate good we must fight for it. Brigham Young said:

Have I any good reason to say to my Father in heaven, "Fight my battles," when he has given me the sword to wield, the arm and the brain that I can fight for myself? Can I ask Him to fight my battles and sit quietly down waiting for Him to do so? I cannot. I can pray the people to hearken to wisdom, to listen to counsel; but to ask God to do for me that which I can do for myself is preposterous to my mind. (*Journal of Discourses* 12:240-41.)

President Young calls the battle against evil "my battle." Each of us should have the same attitude—not the Lord's battle alone but "my battle."

Each of us can profit from the following counsel and exhortation of President Joseph F. Smith:

Shall we quit because there are those with whom we come in contact who are not willing to rise to the standard to which we seek to exalt them? No! Someone has said that the Lord hates a quitter, and there should be no such thing as quitting when we put our hands to the plow to save men, to save souls, to exalt mankind, to inculcate principles of righteousness and establish them in the hearts of those with whom we are associated, both by precept and by example. There must be no such thing as being discouraged. We may fail over and over again, but if we do, it is in individual cases. Under certain conditions and circumstances, we may fail to accomplish the object we have in view with reference to this individual or the other individual, or a number of individuals that we are seeking to benefit, to uplift, to purify, to get into their hearts the principles of justice, of righteousness, of virtue and of honor, that would fit them to inherit the kingdom of God; to associate with angels, should they come to visit the earth. If you fail, never mind. Go right on; try it again; try it somewhere else. Never say quit. Do not say it cannot be done. Failure is a word that should be unknown to all the workers . . . in all the organizations of the Church everywhere. The word "fail" ought to be expunged from our language and our thoughts. . . .

If we continue to try, failing, as it were, or missing one mark, should not discourage us; but we should fly to another, keep on in the work, keep on doing, patiently, determinedly doing our duty, seeking to accomplish the purposes we have in view. (*Gospel Doctrine*, pp. 132-33.)

If we want ultimate peace, ultimate good, we have free agency, and the Lord has invited us to assist him in making it a reality. We have a part in our eventual destiny and in the eventual destiny of mankind.

President Hugh B. Brown has given us this admonition: "We, then, are enlisted in an army with Christ at the head and a living prophet through whom he directs his work. Let us be loyal to them, true to ourselves, and let each of us do the job assigned to him in the place where he is asked to work to the best of his ability." (*Conference Report*, October 1961, p. 86.)

The Lord has said: "For behold, this is my work and my glory—to bring to pass the immortality and eternal life of man." (Moses 1:39.)

Our work and our joy is to assist the Lord. Only those who join him in his great work can be partakers of his great blessings. "The men and women, who desire to obtain seats in the celestial kingdom, will find that they must battle with the enemy of all righteousness every day." (Brigham Young, *Journal of Discourses* 11:14.)

We can overcome Satan and have the power to do so. "The devil is ready to blind our eyes with the things of this world, and he would gladly rob us of eternal life, the greatest of all gifts. But it is not given to the devil, and no power will ever be given to him to overthrow any Latter-day Saint that is keeping the commandments of God. There is no power given to the adversary of men's souls to destroy us if we are doing our duty." (Heber J. Grant, *Conference Report,* October 1900, p. 60.)

We can succeed even if we must do more than our best. With God's help we can do more than our best. Let us consider carefully this counsel from Richard L. Evans:

> May I share with you a sentence or two from Winston Churchill, who said, "It is no use saying 'We are doing our best.' You have got to succeed in doing what is necessary." I'm not sure we know really when we are doing our best. I'm not sure that in most cases we couldn't extend ourselves further in any performance in life. Since eternal life is the great prize, it isn't enough just to try. We have to succeed. There is only one journey—an everlasting one—one time and one eternity—so far as I am aware, and if I may use the vernacular, we can't afford to "sit this one out." Knowing is not enough! (*Improvement Era,* June 1963, p. 474.)

As we reflect upon the friends of our youth and think about how some of them live today, feelings of joy flood our hearts, for many are successful in eternal things. For others we sorrow, because they have departed from the Lord's way and are reaping bitter fruit. We know what separated the faithful from the unfaithful in the scriptures, in Church history, and about us. The faithful ones put on the whole armor of God and kept it on. The unfaithful ones refused to put on the armor or failed to keep it on, and they reap unhappiness here and hereafter. Those who put on the whole armor of God stand firm, help others, and reap God's blessings here and eternally.

"Stand therefore, having your loins girt about with truth, and having on the breastplate of righteousness;

"And your feet shod with the preparation of the gospel of peace;

"Above all, taking the shield of faith, wherewith ye shall be able to quench all the fiery darts of the wicked.

"And take the helmet of salvation, and the sword of the Spirit; which is the word of God:

"Praying always with all prayer and supplication in the Spirit, and watching thereunto with all perseverance and supplication for all saints." (Ephesians 6:14-18.)

Each of us may choose, and, "having done all, . . . stand." (Ephesians 6:13.)

INDEX

72-73; some deny existence of, 93; is perfect, 94; can give us direction, 94; we should honor, in good times and bad, 100; Saints are blessed with knowledge of, 101

Goliath, 46

Good, contrast between evil and, 17

Gospel: prepares men for second coming of christ, 4; commission of Saints to share, 8; should be preached simply, 23; simplicity of principles of, 23-24, 71; is needed by people of all ages, 47

Grant, Heber J.: tells story of John Taylor singing to arguing brethren, 82-83; testimony of daughter of, concerning her mother's death, 100; on limitations to Satan's power, 128

Grant, Jedediah M.: on battling Satan, 85-86; on opposition, 121-22

Habits, influence of, on decisions, 49

Happiness, 122

Harris, Martin, dropped his shield of faith, 60

Harvest, earning of, 51

Having done all, definition of, 119

Heart: purity of, 31, 33; Christ asks us to give our, 33-34; hardness of, 35; change of, 35-36; determines actions, 36; protection of, with breastplate of righteousness, 38; being of one, 41

Heaven, one-third of hosts of, were cast out, 14

Helaman, teachings of, on word of God, 89-90

Helmet: of salvation, protects mind, 67; description of Roman, 67-68; of salvation, purposes served by, 75; should be examined periodically for holes, 76; price of securing in place, 76

Hinckley, Alonzo A., gift of tongues of, 83-84

Holy Ghost: is Spirit of truth, 24, 30; Christ promised, to his disciples, 30; role of, 30; teachers must teach with, 80-81; words spoken under influence of, are from God, 81; testimony of, touched Brigham Young, 81-82; helped missionary bear testimony in Dutch, 84

Humility, 34-35

Hymns, John Taylor sang, to arguing brethren, 82-83

Immorality, 23

Inspiration of heroic deeds, 4

Intelligence: glory of God is, 75; depends on protection of helmet of salvation, 75-76

Jesus Christ: appeared to Joseph and Sidney in vision, 11; becoming like, 18; was born to bear witness of truth, 19; is the way, the truth, and the life, 20, 73; communicates simply, 21; washed feet of disciples, 34; peace of, 44; redeemed men from the fall, 45-46; influence of, on tax collector, 55; adulterous woman taken before, 55; salvation comes through, 56, 75; role of, in plan of salvation, 69-70;

Obedience: is companion to simplicity, 23; blessings depend on, 99

"Oh say, what is truth?" hymn, 29

Opposition, 121; in all things, 56; reason for, 69

Others, caring more for, than for self, 113

Paul: was Roman citizen, 5; instructed Saints to put on God's armor, 5

Peace: of Christ, 44; must begin internally, 49, 52

Perfection: improvement toward, 24; of God, 94

Perseverance in face of persecution, 110, 112

Peter counseled Saints to be vigilant, 13

Philosophy, difficulty in understanding of, 22

Pilate, 19

Plan: definition of, 57-58; of God, 58

Planting, time for, 51

Potiphar, wife of, 26

Pratt, Parley P.: prayed for money to cross lake, 101; desire of, to serve God, 122

Prayer: importance of, to Daniel, 91-92; of Marriner W. Merrill, 92; Christ emphasized and taught, 94-96; should not be self-centered, 96; should be refreshing, 96; persistence in, 96-97; of David O. McKay for testimony, 98; separate, for each day and task, 98-99; is a privilege, 99; in specific terms, 101; of Parley P. Pratt, 101; John Taylor's reliance on, 102; methods of answering, 103-4; Brigham

Young's advice to his son concerning, 104; unity in, 104-5; of mother for her son in the service, 109

Premortal existence, 69

Preparation: likened to putting on boots, 44; emphasis on, in Roman army, 44; example of, at scene of accident, 45; lack of, 45, 47; eliminates fear, 45; methods of, 49-50; one form of, is making right decisions, 52

Pride: preaching of false doctrines due to, 74; leads to apostasy, 76

Principles, basic, we should teach only, 21

Procrastination, 48, 71-73

Prophet, we must follow, 115, 127

Purity of heart, 31, 33

Qualities, acquiring of needed, 61

Rameumptom, 111

Recognition: worldly, relative unimportance of, 61-62; learning not to need, 125

Recreation, standards of, 24

Repentance, labor in crying, 18

Resurrection, 70

Revelations: are made to be understood, 21-22; language of, men attempted to imitate, 22; concerning God's methods of answering prayers, 103-4. See also Word of God

Rigdon, Sidney: saw God, Christ, and Lucifer in vision, 12; was encompassed by Satan, 13

Righteousness: definition of, 31; produces pure hearts, 36

Rules should not be constantly questioned, 58-59

Jesus was simple, 21; should be simple and intelligible, 23; with Holy Ghost, 80

Telestial kingdom, 71

Temptation, truth protects against, 26

Terrestrial kingdom, 70-71

Testimony: loss of, 3; of Joseph and Sidney, 11; prayer of David O. McKay for, 98; listening to others bear, helped author decide to go on mission, 116-18

Tests: of each individual, 61; recognition of, as such, 123

Thompson, Robert, 66

Thoughts determine actions, 36

Tithing, simplicity of principle of, 23

Tongues, story of missionary blessed with gift of, 83-84

Treasure, definition of, 81

Truth: armor of, 19; definition of, 19; shall make you free, 20; Holy Ghost is Spirit of, 24; living by, 24; protects against temptation, 26; will bring ultimate victory, 27; protects chastity, 28

Unity in prayer, 104-5

Vanity, departure from simplicity brings, 24

Vigilance: advised by Peter, 13; in holding up shield of faith, 63; can never be relaxed, 119

Vision: of Father and Son, given to Joseph and Sidney, 11-12; of Satan and his followers, by Joseph Smith, 16-17

War: to save souls, 13; against Satan's angels, 14; Christ's prediction of, 45

Waving goodbye, story of, 2

Whittier, John Greenleaf, quotation by, 60

Williams, Frederick G., 3

Wine was not to be purchased from enemies, 6

Woodruff, Wilford: on Satan's angels, 14; on apostasy of Church leaders, 74-75; baptized constable sent to arrest him, 86-87

Word of God: is used in variety of ways, 79, 89; men must obtain, through study, 81; must be used right in each situation, 83; leads to exaltation, 89-90

World, Christ's disciples are not of, 44

Works must accompany faith, 56

Yard, story of couple cleaning up neighbor's, 37

Young, Brigham: departing for mission, 1-2; on war for righteousness, 14, 128; on Joseph Smith's teaching abilities, 20-21; on testimony given with power of Holy Ghost, 81-82; advises his son to pray, 104; on love of the cause of God, 122; on asking God to do what we could do for ourselves, 126

Young, Mary Ann (wife of Brigham), 2

Zacchaeus, 55

Zoramites, 110-11